"Your Majesties, this is Kate Smith—this is America."

With these words President Roosevelt introduced the favorite singing star of the country to King George VI and Queen Elizabeth. The year was 1939. Less than ten years earlier, guided by her knowledgeable manager, Ted Collins, Kate Smith had begun her career in radio. And less than five years before that—at the age of seventeen—knowing only that she was gifted with a beautiful voice and that she must sing, Kate Smith had left her native Washington, D. C. A singing-dancing part in a Broadway musical comedy of the Twenties seemed a promising first step to the ambitious young girl. But instead of glamour and success, she endured four years of loneliness and unhappiness as the butt of fat-girl jokes ad-libbed by second-rate comedians. And despair and disappointment accompanied the realization that it was her appearance and not her talent that had won her the role.

It was then that Ted Collins, a talent scout for Columbia Records, asked her to record for him, beginning a lifelong partnership unique

The tremendous loyalty of manager-partner was never onstrated than when Collins attack in 1956. Kate imme- all scheduled engagements ake public appearances until o be present during her per- only after his recovery that :ing guest appearances and [V show.

Her contributions to public welfare have been remarkable. She sold 600 million dollars' worth of bonds during World War II, raised four million dollars for a Red Cross emergency flood relief fund, and has tirelessly aided a multitude of charities.

Kate Smith is a person to whom the years have brought peace and enjoyment of life. Not a glamour girl, never involved in sensational or romantic headlines, she is a hard-headed, realistic woman who knows what she wants and, more important, how to get it. She is a woman with whom people feel comfort-
views on religion, marriage versus
life, a career, and the business of
living have been conditioned by
: and success. And her music and
f life have remained free of preten-
.ffected by fads of the day.

UPON MY LIPS A SONG is Kate Smith's own story. It is as inspiring as it is American.

Upon My Lips A Song

Kate Smith

Upon My Lips A Song

3

Because the road was steep and long
And through a dark and lonely land,
God set upon my lips a song
And put a lantern in my hand.

JOYCE KILMER

*I hereby acknowledge my indebtedness to
Ruth Mitchell Van Zuyle for her assistance
in the writing of this book.*

Upon My Lips A Song

One

 $\mathcal{T}$ HINKING it over since then, it has always seemed strange to me that when the telephone rang in my apartment on that Sunday afternoon in January four years ago, it sounded the same as it has always sounded. Quite illogically, I feel that its ring should have had some foreboding note in it, something to warn me that it was bringing me the worst shock I have ever had.

But it did not. Indeed, everything about that afternoon was deceptively normal. It was one of those rare January afternoons when the sun shines with a pale brilliance, lighting up one side of the street and plunging the other into dark shadow. My apartment is high up in a building on Park Avenue. From the window, when I looked up, I could see the sky, a very pale blue with white fluffy clouds blown along, and when I looked down I could see the people in the street sauntering in the lazy tempo of a New York Sunday. My mother and I were sitting by the window, enjoying the sunshine and watching the activity below. Occasionally, with a Sunday languor, a bus would come along, draw to the curb briefly, and then swing out again; a taxi would sweep through the traffic with an ease impossible on any other day.

My mother, who was then about seventy years old and had a lot of curly gray-white hair which caught the rays of the sun, was chatting with me about some friends whom we had asked to the apartment that evening to play a few hands of bridge. Among them was Phyllis, who had been in nurses' training with me years before in Washington, and who was now a much sought-after private nurse in New York, and Barbara, a neighborhood friend who had grown up with the Smith girls in Washington and later married and settled in New York. Barbara's daughter was going to be married next month, and my mother and I were discussing what we should give her for a wedding present. It was an idle, laughing, relaxed conversation. I have always enjoyed Sunday because there is time for this kind of talk. We had been to church that morning, and the measured beauty of the service contributed to our serenity.

And then the telephone rang. It shattered the peace of that afternoon just as surely as if the house had blown up.

But I didn't realize it at that moment. I thought the

4

caller would be one of my friends to tell me that perhaps she would be late arriving, or would like to bring another guest. So I told Mother I would answer it, and went on talking to her as I crossed the room. The telephone stood on a small table near the door and there was a straight chair next to it.

I knew something was wrong when I picked up the receiver and heard the voice of Dr. Garlan say "Hello." Dr. Garlan had been physician to me and to my manager, Ted Collins, for many years.

"Miss Smith," he said, "I have some very bad news for you. Ted has had a heart attack."

"Is he d——?" I began to say in a curiously normal voice.

"No, he isn't dead, but he is very ill indeed."

I sat down on the hard chair next to the telephone table. Slowly, as the news sank in, I began to cry. I heard my mother get up from her chair at the window and cross to my side. My hands began to shake and my mouth went dry. Questions began pouring into my mind and I tried to ask them all at once.

"Dr. Garlan, how did it happen? Where is he? Can I see him? What shall I do?"

Dr. Garlan's voice remained firm. "Please try to keep calm. He's in Doctors' Hospital——"

"I'll go up there right away——" I began.

"No, please don't. Ted is now in an oxygen tent, and since he's under very heavy sedation, he wouldn't know you were there."

5

"When did it happen?"

"It happened earlier this afternoon at his apartment. A friend was visiting him and they were talking about his football teams, when he suddenly collapsed on the floor. The friend called me and as soon as I saw him I sent for an ambulance and we got him to the hospital."

"How bad is it, Doctor?"

Dr. Garlan hesitated a moment. "I don't have to tell you lies. It is a severe coronary thrombosis. He's very, very ill."

"Can't I go up and see him?" I asked again.

"Better wait until the morning. You can't do anything for him and you don't want to be in the nurses' way, do you? Look, I'm going back to the hospital now. I'll call you tonight near nine to tell you about his condition. And if anything happens——" I caught my breath, but he repeated the phrase, "if anything happens, I shall call you at once."

"But there must be something I can do."

"Miss Smith, there is nothing you can do except wait. That's what we're all doing. And please don't get yourself so upset that I have to come and give you a sedative. You're a strong woman, and you won't help by giving way to weakness."

"All right. I'll wait for your call. And please let me see him soon!" I heard him say good-by as I put the telephone down.

For a long while I sat without moving, my mother's arm on my shoulder. The tears dried in patches where I

6

had smeared them on my cheeks, and I stared into space, trying to comprehend the reality of the fact that Ted Collins was lying in a hospital bed in grave danger. The first shock of the news was over. Now there was a numbness, a disbelief, a feeling that I had dreamed it all.

My mother gently urged me to come and sit beside her on the sofa. As we crossed the room I noticed, quite irrelevantly, that the sun had gone down behind the tall buildings and there was only one ray lighting up the draperies. Soon that too would be gone.

As we sat down, the numbness was replaced by a sharp pain, the pain of grief. I began to weep quietly, feeling as if my heart would break. "Mother, why did it have to happen to Ted?"

"Kathryn, no one knows that. It can happen to any-body, you know. But the worst hasn't happened yet and we can pray that it won't."

We sat silent for a little while longer, until my mother apologetically reminded me that we had invited guests and if we were going to ask them not to come, we should do so as soon as possible. I begged her to tele-phone and tell them what had happened; I knew that they would want to come anyway, but I couldn't face even that.

Mother got up to telephone Phyllis and Barbara and the others, while I remained on the sofa, my thoughts far away. I could feel her talking quietly in the back-ground, but I didn't hear her; I heard Ted's voice as I

7

had heard it for twenty-six years, explaining, cajoling, shouting, laughing, a cascade of phrases tumbling in my head. Above and in front of them all was one question: what if I should never hear that voice again?

The relationship between Ted Collins and myself has never been the ordinary one between a manager and a singer. If it had been, my grief at his heart attack would have been as sharp, but not as deep. Ted was more than a manager, more even than a friend; to explain his closeness to me is difficult using the ordinary terms of relationship. Without Ted there would have been no Kate Smith—the Kate Smith the public has known for almost thirty years.

Our partnership is unique in show business in that we have never had a written contract. Our unwritten contract is based on Ted's complete faith in my talent and my complete trust in his interest and judgment. Our business partnership is unique. Our friendship is unique.

I relied on Ted Collins so completely that I often didn't know what shows he had signed up for until we went into rehearsal, for I knew I could trust him to do what was best for us. Before the heart attack occurred, I had heard vaguely that we were to do some guest appearances on television, but as usual, I had left all the details to Ted. We had retired from our regular daily television program in 1954, but we were still making many guest appearances.

This was the background of my thoughts as I struggled to accept and understand what had happened.

Mother had finished telephoning and returned to the sofa. She put her hand on mine and said, "Kathryn, everyone is very sympathetic and they're all praying for Ted. Would you like some coffee if I made it? You should have something."

"No, thanks," I answered. "I couldn't swallow anything now. I think I'll go to my room." I wanted to pray for Ted. There's a time when prayer needs solitude.

"Don't you want to go up to St. Patrick's? We could go while they're singing Vespers," Mother said gently.

"No, it's Sunday and the cathedral will be full of people. I just don't want to see anyone or have anyone look at me, to be truthful." The tears welled up in my eyes again. "I'm sure God will understand," I said as I walked to my bedroom. I heard Mother sit down again and knew she, too, would pray. Ted had been her friend also. How often he had made her laugh!

All during the years of my daily radio program I had found myself frequently in the position of trying to offer comfort to people who had suffered losses, particularly during the war. I felt completely inadequate myself to help mothers whose sons had been killed, or who had heard they were missing, so I always advised them to seek help from God, in whatever way they worshipped. I had so often told them there was no substitute for religion in time of trouble. I had so often answered the question, "What can I do?" with, "You can always pray."

Now, at this time of crisis in my own life, I was to

feel as I had never felt before the value of prayer and of taking troubles to God. He would hear my prayers with love and understanding.

Sitting in the armchair by my four-poster bed I opened the Bible at a marked passage and read:

"Come unto me, all ye that labor and are heavy laden, and I will give you rest. Take my yoke upon you and learn of me, for I am lowly in heart and ye shall find rest unto your souls."

I put the book down and slipped to my knees at the side of the bed.

As nine o'clock approached, both Mother and I began to glance nervously at the clock and then at the telephone. Mercifully no one had called us since the doctor had broken the news; I don't know if I could have picked up the receiver. My fear of perhaps hearing the worst news of all was too great.

It was a few minutes before nine when the telephone rang. The sound of Dr. Garlan's voice gave courage to my hopes.

"There has been no turn for the worse. Ted is resting comfortably now and is doing as well as can be expected." As well as can be expected. Those who have heard those words understand how much they mean, and how little.

"Is there any more hope for his recovery, Doctor?"

"That I can't tell you. He's holding his own, but no one can predict what the night will bring."

"May I see him tomorrow?"

"Yes, I think so. I'll call you very early in the morning and tell you how he passed the night."

"Couldn't I call the hospital myself and ask them?" I urged. The terror of waiting all night, not knowing, seemed too much.

"You could, but it would only inconvenience them. Please, Miss Smith, leave it to me and to the hospital staff. Everything possible is being done. Now you get a good night's sleep."

"All right, Doctor. Thank you."

A "good night's sleep" was an impossibility, almost an impertinence. Mother and I sat in the living room together until long after midnight, talking only occasionally. My mind was working so hard at picturing Ted as I had always known him that I soon found it impossible to move to go to bed. It was as if there was a theater in my head and I was watching a beloved performer acting out a life, going through scene after scene until there was a sudden click, and the actor slumped to the floor and was carried off the stage. Again and again the drama was acted out, always with the same terrible ending. My imagination seemed to be trying to force a different ending each time the scenes were played through, but it was never possible, and there was never anything beyond the slumped figure on the floor. I couldn't make it rise again, I couldn't hear it speak in the old tones; it remained still until it was moved.

When at last Mother insisted I go to my room, I knelt by my bed for at least another hour. Now I was praying that Ted would be spared through the night, a time which is always more critical than the day for the sick. I wanted so much to see him, to wipe out the picture of the slumped figure on the floor and replace it with another.

Sleep at last came through sheer exhaustion as I lay staring into the darkness, the same drama running over and over again in my head. But as I slept fitfully, the play changed. It became now a horror of the telephone, so that I woke time and time again feeling absolutely certain it was ringing, bringing me the worst news; but as I listened in the dark, there was no ring. Only an awful stillness. Then I fell asleep again and saw the telephone getting bigger and bigger, puffing up like a balloon filled with air, until it filled the room and threatened to crush me in bed. And just as it was about to do so, it began ringing again, a ring so loud that its sound nearly deafened me. I awoke with a start, and the perspiration soaked my face. There was no sound.

Again I slept and this time I wanted to keep on calling people myself, to keep the telephone busy, so that the fatal ringing would never be heard. I saw myself calling Phyllis and Barbara and many others, talking, talking, talking to them at the top of my voice, gabbing about anything, anything, so long as the phone could not ring.

As soon as I put the receiver down, I would immediately dial a new number, and begin the hysterical chatter all over again, fighting desperately never to let the dreadful call through.

I don't know how long I must have half-slept in this state, but when I awoke it was eight o'clock by the antique French clock on my dressing table—and the phone was ringing. Curiously enough, it did not send me into a panic; I had become so familiar with the sound in my dreams that it had lost its power now that it was a reality.

When I lifted the receiver of the extension which was on my bedside table, I heard the gentle voice of Minnie, Ted's secretary for many years. She told me how sorry she was to hear about Ted's illness.

"Isn't it dreadful, Minnie? I don't know what to do. How did you find out?" I asked.

"Dr. Garlan just called me here at home," she answered. "What are we going to do about the newspapers?"

"I don't know, Minnie." I was about to add automatically, "Ted will look after that," when I realized that for the first time in twenty-six years, he couldn't. Tears welled in me again.

"Minnie, what will we do without him? I don't know what to say to the papers or to anyone."

"It's all right, Miss Smith, I won't do anything about them. When they find out, I suppose we could get Dr. Garlan to give a statement, but we won't do anything ourselves. And what shall I do if Mr. Sullivan's office calls?"

"Mr. Sullivan?" I asked.

"Yes, you're supposed to be appearing on the Ed Sullivan show on the twenty-ninth. What shall I do about it?"

The thought of appearing on any show at any time was the furthest thing from my mind. What should I do? Oh, why wasn't Ted here to do these things for me?

"I don't know what you should say to him. Just tell him Ted's very ill and I have no idea what's going to happen."

I put the phone down and leaned back on the pillow. The thought of Ted's death hovered around me but I fought to ignore its presence. Mother came in with a cup of coffee for me. I tried to sip it, but the cup teetered in my trembling hands. Mother went to the window and pulled open the Venetian blinds, letting in the pale light of a gray New York day.

At long last, Dr. Garlan called. I handed the tray to Mother as I picked up the receiver. I hardly gave him the opportunity to say hello. "Doctor, how is he?"

"He's holding his own. I've just been to see him, and he was resting as peacefully as we can expect. There's been no recurrence."

"May I go to see him today?"

"Yes, I've arranged with the hospital for you to see him this morning. You won't be able to speak to him or spend much time there; you can just go in and see him briefly. I'll be there to meet you. Come at about ten-thirty. Is that all right?"

"Thank you so much, Doctor, I'll be there."

I went to Doctors' Hospital alone. Usually I very much enjoy driving through New York streets because I love the quick glimpses of the features on the face of the city. The people, the shop windows, the cab driver's opinions. But this time I could have been driving through a frightening silent desert for all I saw or heard. My ears were still directed inward.

At the door of the hospital Dr. Garlan's tall figure was standing ready to greet me. He is a man with a marvelous gift of quiet confidence in time of crisis; his smile and handshake communicated something of his calm to me, although I could not smile in reply. Once inside the hospital the atmosphere almost choked me; the over-heated air and the mingled smells of disinfectants and medicines combined with the shining floors and the whiteness of walls, doors and uniforms to fill me with the worst foreboding. Whenever I smell that peculiarly stuffy smell of a hospital now, I always remember that morning, the ride up in the elevator, the walk along the corridors, and finally, the door to Ted's room.

Outside I was introduced to other doctors and nurses who were looking after Ted, and Dr. Garlan whispered to me, "Be prepared for a shock, Miss Smith. He doesn't look well. We won't stay too long, because there's nothing we can do right now."

Ted's bed was against the left wall of the room as we

entered, and a nurse was sitting on the side nearest to us with the cylinders of oxygen. At first I could see nothing but the plastic of the oxygen tent, for the room was in semi-darkness with the shades down. I crossed to the other side and came close to the bed.

In spite of Dr. Garlan's warning, I couldn't repress an anguished gasp. I could hardly believe this was Ted. He looked so small, as if the heart attack had drained from him not only his strength but also his bulk. His face, which is usually round and made rounder with a habitual smile, seemed hollow as he slept, as if the flesh had dropped away. The lines on it, which had been remarkably few, now looked as if they had been etched into the very bone and the shadows made blacker with pencil. Through the plastic tent he looked gray against the white pillow. It was obvious that he was breathing uncertainly and with more than effort.

His head moved occasionally and his hands, near the bottom of the plastic cover, moved nervously. I thought at first he was trying to get the tent away from him, as though it were worrying him, but I soon realized that he was so deep in his drugged sleep that the actions must have been reflexes and not conscious.

The room was so warm that I had to slip off my coat as I sat in the chair beside the bed, opposite the nurse, who smiled calmly at me. There was very little noise except for the subdued hissing of the oxygen cylinder and the hum of traffic outside the window in the street below. Dr. Garlan was examining some charts. The door opened, and another doctor in a white coat came in, looked at me, went to Dr. Garlan's side and began talking to him softly.

I looked again and again at the figure on the bed. This was the image that was to replace the slumped body in my mental pictures for many weeks to come. There was hardly more hope, hardly more comfort in it. Could I believe that this figure any more than the other one would eventually get up, snap into color and action and become Ted? He looked so frail lying there, and the irregularity of his breathing seemed only a few moments from not breathing at all.

Dr. Garlan turned to me. "Shall we go now?" he whispered gently. I nodded, unable to speak, and put on my coat with his help. With one last unbelieving glance at Ted's helpless figure, I walked out with Dr. Garlan.

Outside I could not restrain my tears and had to fumble for a handkerchief. Dr. Garlan led me to the elevator. Downstairs, he made me sit down on a sofa in the lobby with him. He remained patiently silent until I stopped crying.

"Doctor, I've never seen anything like it. How could a man like Ted be changed so suddenly into that . . . that . . ."

"Heart attacks are terrible things, and people who've had no previous experience with them are always horrified at their effects. But people don't take the right steps to avoid them and they keep on happening," he said.

"What hope is there that Ted will . . . will live through this?" I asked.

"I simply couldn't tell you. All we can do is watch him day and night and hope that with the correct treatment his heart will mend. He is progressing satisfactorily now, but I don't know how long he will need the sedation or the oxygen tent. Quite honestly, I think we're lucky he's here now."

"How long will it be before he can speak to me?"

"I have to keep telling you, Miss Smith, I don't know. But I'm quite sure you'll be the first person he will talk to when he can," he said with a patient smile.

"What caused it, Doctor?" I was looking for something on which to blame the horror of it all.

"A coronary thrombosis is caused by excessive strain on the heart. What the strain itself is caused by can vary. Ted is a man who lived and worked under great pressure —I don't need to tell you that." He smiled.

"No, I suppose you don't. And I suppose that while I was singing or talking over radio and television he was worrying about all the details I never even thought about." Had I found the right person to blame for it?

Dr. Garlan turned squarely to me and said firmly, "Miss Smith, this is not your fault nor the fault of any one person. You must forget thoughts of that kind entirely and concentrate on keeping yourself hopeful. Come along, you must go home now. You can come again tomorrow, but not if you're going to cry." He stood up and smiled at me. I got to my feet with his assistance, and asked him to call me in the afternoon to tell me about Ted's condition. He promised he would.

I did not go home. I went to St. Patrick's Cathedral on Fifth Avenue. There I slipped in through the side door, hoping that no one would recognize me, and went straight to the Chapel of Our Lady of New York with her sweet face bathed in the soft blue light which sifted from the stained glass window above her. There was a musky smell of incense mingled with the slightly smoky fragrance of the many candles flickering before the altars of the saints on either side of the main body of the Cathedral. Here, I thought, if anywhere, in this sacred structure where God is worshipped according to rituals which have hardly changed in nearly two thousand years, where people have brought their troubles and bewilderment and have found help, here I too shall find comfort.

As I sat there, another verse from the Bible came into my mind. I had learned it as a child, and often repeated it, but now its full significance came to me.

"And I say unto you, ask, and it shall be given you; seek, and ye shall find; knock and it shall be opened unto you. For every one that asketh, receiveth; and he that seeketh, findeth; and unto him that knocketh it shall be opened. And of which of you that is a father shall his son ask a loaf, and he give him a stone? Or a fish, and he for a fish give him a serpent? Or if he shall ask an egg, will he give him a scorpion? If ye, then, being evil, know how to give good gifts unto your children, how much more shall your heavenly Father give the Holy Spirit to them that ask him?"

"Ask and it shall be given you . . ." I knelt again and looked earnestly at the face of Mary. I asked her to intercede for me in my request, and prayed to her as the Mother of God. I asked her, as one who had known suffering, to spare Ted for his sake and my own. I told her that I would come twice a day to pray for his life, and if he got well, I would come twice a day for a whole year to glorify her name.

I told Our Lady that I would not sing again until Ted was at my side, and that if he should not recover, I would never sing again. This was hardly a vow, since I knew that it would be almost physically impossible for me to sing without Ted. Whenever I sang, it was as much to justify his great faith and pride in me as to please any audience. I was sure that without him to listen no sound could come easily from my heart. Ours had perhaps been a duet. "I'll carry the problems, Kathryn," Ted had often said, "you carry the tune." But I never could have sung alone. I remained on my knees praying silently and earnestly for a long time. I walked slowly out of the Cathedral. I was reluctant to leave the place of hope—the hope that I saw in Dr. Garlan's eyes had so uncertain a foundation.

When I went to bed that night I was calmer but could not sleep for many long hours. I suddenly realized how alone I would be if Ted died; I would have no heart for work. I would never again walk out on a stage and wait for those always exciting opening bars before my songs—a bleak prospect for anyone like me who had spent her life in the bustling world of show business. I began to feel cold and alone as I thought of it. Suppose that at this very moment the figure I had seen in the white, antiseptic room was struggling to draw one more breath—and couldn't quite make it?

For the next week—I think it was a week—I was almost unconscious of the passing of time. I went to St. Patrick's Cathedral morning and afternoon to kneel before the statue of Our Lady of New York, and I went to see Ted. He was always the same, and the doctors still could not give any assurance that he would eventually win out in the struggle he was putting up against death. Dr. Garlan called me three times daily to give me news, and whenever the telephone rang at other times I had to steel myself to answer it.

My fantasies swung between hope and despair. At times I could imagine Ted, out of the oxygen tent and sitting up in bed, saying, "Hello, Kathryn," in that warm sincere voice of his. At other times I saw him still and motionless, and a cold breath chilled my face. At those times I suppose I cried as much for myself left alone as for Ted. Grief has unavoidably a large amount of self-pity in it, and although it may seem inappropriate, it is in fact a tribute to the person for whom one grieves.

Minnie called several times during the week to ask

how Ted was and to worry with me. Finally, on Monday, she said almost apologetically, "Miss Smith, we're going to have to do something about the newspapers today because they'll want to know why you're not on the Ed Sullivan Show next Sunday."

"Oh, Minnie," I answered without any idea of what we ought to say to the newspapers. "Why don't you ask Dr. Garlan to give out a statement about Ted's condition? Won't that be enough?"

"Well, can I add that you won't sing until he's better?" she asked gently. I was grateful for her confidence that he would get better.

"Yes, yes, do that," I told her. I had never in my career given a statement to the press without Ted, but Minnie had often done it under his directions.

Minnie told me later that after the news appeared in the afternoon papers, her office was deluged with phone calls inquiring about Ted, letters and cards from friends, and gifts of all kinds intended to cheer an invalid. But he couldn't yet be called even an "invalid"; he was still somewhere on the shaky ground between life and death.

One afternoon I came back from visiting the hospital and the Cathedral full of despair. It seemed to me that by now there should be some improvement, if there was ever going to be any, and yet he had appeared exactly the same. No change, at least to my searching eyes. I sat down near the window and looked up at the sky, which remained impassively gray. My mother made tea, and we drank it in silence. Afterward I sat for a long time staring at my empty cup. The only way I can describe how I felt is to say that I seemed to be at the end of a dark street, faced by an immovable wall. I felt helpless.

Mother and I began quietly to talk about my years with Ted. We both of us had a store of memories of him, and it was like turning the leaves of an album as one of us spoke of an incident and then the other added to it and went on to another. There were long periods of silence between us. During one of these I suddenly became aware that there had been a time when there was no Ted—and it was a time when I had been very unhappy. I said to Mother, "You never knew how unhappy I was when I first came to New York, did you? I told you a little about it, but I don't think anyone but myself knew the extent of it."

"Why do you think of that now?" she asked.

"Because it's the last time I can remember feeling as much despair as I do now. Oh, of course, the despair is different in kind, because I was very young then, but it was very nearly as acute."

In the silence I saw myself again as I had been before Ted came into my life.

Two

S O M E W H E R E near my hotel window on Forty-second Street in that summer of 1926 there must have been an advertising sign which flashed on and off again in red, for at night a red gleam regularly lit up the dressing table and as regularly plunged the room into a luminous semi-darkness. It was never completely dark there for the lights of Forty-second Street went off only as dawn replaced them.

I could have pulled the shade down, but I had tried that once and all but suffocated. I now opened the window in the hope of catching whatever breeze there might be. The air was as hot and sticky as a steam bath, and my room on the ninth floor seemed to have accumulated all the heat and staleness of the eight floors below. The open window admitted an occasional feeble breeze, and all the noise of the street as well. Cars, which in those days had louder engines than they do now, seemed to be going up and down Forty-second Street all night long. Sometimes their brakes screeched. An angry taxi driver would honk insistently at someone in his way, and gears ground and clashed. Occasionally there would be the sound of raised voices; shrieks of laughter would float up to my window as parties of gay young women, wearing skirts above their knees and long strings of beads, went by with their escorts.

I tossed on my bed and tried to shut out the noises in another attempt to sleep. I took a handkerchief from the bedside table, the top of which was pitted with cigarette burns, and wiped some of the sticky dampness from my face. The pillow was wet and warm; the sheet I lay on stuck to my back above my nightgown, which was crumpled and clammy too. I had been lying there for at least two hours and had not yet succeeded in sleeping; my nerves were strained by the light in the room and the incessant noises. I longed for a dark room with a light breeze, to drift into that deep sleep you can almost drink with pleasure.

I turned again until I lay on my back, groaning with sheer exasperation. It must have been about midnight. My watch was on the dressing table across the room, but I was too drained to get up and look at it. Every time the red sign flashed on, a ray lit up the gold of my watch so that it gleamed like a tiny pilot light.

Now the nerves of my legs began to twitch as they felt the strain of having danced the Charleston over and over again at rehearsal that day. I moved my legs to a different position but they would not rest; they were still jumping and kicking as they had been for nearly three hours on the stage of a deserted theater on Broadway. My face broke out in more perspiration as I thought of having to dance like that again the next day —and the next. My head was aching, not only with tiredness and the effect of physical discomfort, but with hunger too; no one in the company of "Honeymoon Lane" had asked me to join the group for dinner and I hadn't been able to face eating alone. Instead I had come back to this bare, suffocating room, written a letter to my mother and gone to bed, hoping to sleep away my troubles.

My eyes wandered slowly around the little room, as they had done for a number of nights now. I hadn't slept soundly since I came to New York, and every spot on the wallpaper was well known to me. The room was too small and had been used by too many people before me without being redecorated. There was an ink stain on the wall beside the table, a round blotch with long rivulets running to the floor. In one corner stood the washbasin, which was coming away from the wall. A faucet dripped, adding its bit of torture to my strained nerves. I shared a bathroom down the hall with another member of the cast of "Honeymoon Lane," and was revolted every day by the ring left around the tub. I wondered how many other young girls who had great thoughts of success on Broadway had occupied this room, and whether they too had found its dreariness almost more than they could bear.

It was so impersonal—that was what I could not take. It held no welcome for me when I opened the door, it did not feel like "my" room. It seemed to say nothing to me, not to care whether I slept or couldn't sleep. There was nothing in it to which I could turn for comfort when I came back hot and tired. It was almost a symbol of the new life I had just entered. It was not going to help me in any way; it shrugged its shoulders and said, "You've got to be tough to take it."

As I looked up at the dirty, flaking ceiling I asked myself if I was really tough enough, at the age of seventeen, to conquer Broadway. Perhaps I should have waited, turned down the opportunity to be Tiny Little, and hoped for another part later. A wave of homesickness filled me: if only my mother were here to encourage me! In my letter I had told her about the rehearsals and the theater, but I hadn't dared to admit that I couldn't sleep, didn't really eat enough and that I wanted her comforting presence so much.

The red light flashed on again and through my tears I saw the gold of my watch catch its rays. It became a focus for my thoughts. It reminded me of something;

with the help of memory, it became part of a scene from my childhood.

It was a Sunday evening just after Christmas about ten years earlier. The whole family was gathered in the living room of our home in Washington, D.C. Candlelight reflected on my mother's rich golden hair as she sat at the piano playing Christmas carols. The candles stood on top of the piano, shedding a soft light on the heavy furniture and dark colors of the room. There was an atmosphere of quiet happiness; we were all singing carols, and the harmonies were simple and pleasing.

Besides my mother and father and sister Helene, my maternal grandparents, Granny and Grandpa Hanby, were there. They were present on all occasions like Christmas and Easter and our birthdays; whenever I think of my home I see them there as well as my parents.

In the corner of the room stood a small Christmas tree, decorated with gay ornaments, and next to the tree, in an armchair, sat Granny Hanby, with my sister Helene on a small stool at her feet. Granny Hanby was a small, plump woman of very upright carriage; even when she sat in an armchair, her back was as straight as a ramrod. Her hair was neatly coiled into a gray bun at the back of her head, and she wore steel-rimmed spectacles. Her expression, which was softened by the candlelight, was usually a little severe, for she believed in discipline and order in life. When she looked at her Smith granddaughters, however, her eyes were nearly always kind.

My father stood beside the piano, turning the pages

for Mother as she played. On the red sofa by the door sat Grandpa Hanby, who was a tall and very distinguished-looking man. He had a long face with a prominent nose and very white hair; it was still wavy and sat like a plume on his head. Like Granny, he wore steel-rimmed glasses, and when he was dressed for visiting, as he was now, he wore a vest with a watch and chain. I must have played with the shiny watch many times as a baby, and it still fascinated me. It was so solemn and round, and had that air of being sacred that older people's possessions very often have for children. I was looking at it then, as I stood at the end of the sofa, twisting my fingers in the hem of my dress while we all sang together.

My sister and I both had our hair in long braids with big bows of white ribbon at the ends. Our dresses were white with elaborate ruffles and broad sashes around the waist. Our mother and grandmother, of course, wore long skirts, and their faces had never known powder.

As we came to the end of a carol, there was a rustling and shuffling as Granny and Grandpa got back their breath, smiling and laughing at mother. She turned to Father and asked, "What shall it be now?"

"Let's ask Kathryn to sing to us. She's got more breath than we have," he answered. "I don't think Granny and Grandpa have heard her sing 'Away in a Manger' this year, have they?"

I needed no second bidding, for I have never known stage-fright at any time. Father brought out a little footstool that stood in front of a high-backed chair at the window, and put it beside the piano for me to stand on. He sat down beside Grandpa, while I stood up very straight, smoothing down my dress with my hands. Mother nodded her head as she sounded the first chord; I sang as well as I knew how, thoroughly enjoying both the song and the audience.

When I had finished, there was a little silence, and then my grandfather said softly, "That was lovely, Kathryn." Helene clapped her hands, while mother looked at me with a bright smile of pride.

Granny Hanby said, "Come here, Kathryn, and let me kiss you." She put her arm around me and kissed my cheek. I noticed that there were tears in her eyes, but I couldn't imagine why she should be crying.

The scene faded as the red light went out once more. I felt even more alone by contrast with that warm family circle where it was impossible to feel unwanted.

I turned over and buried my face in the pillow, trying to blot out the picture; I knew if I thought about it any more I should get so miserable that I'd probably give it all up and go back home. To forget it, I tried to recite my lines from "Honeymoon Lane." I mentally rehearsed them in several different ways, trying to find the one which would please the director most.

But my efforts were thwarted by voices that I had heard earlier in the day and every day since I had joined the cast of "Honeymoon Lane." I heard the voice of a boy in the chorus greeting me as I arrived in the morning with "Hello, Fatty." I heard someone else say as we bought doughnuts and coffee at a stand, "Betcha she buys a dozen doughnuts and a gallon o' coffee."

A photographer had come to take pictures to put in the theater foyer during the afternoon, and as I posed doing the Charleston, someone shouted to the cameraman, "Can you get her all on one plate?"

They didn't seem to realize that I was a singer, and that I was in the show because I wanted to sing. I enjoyed the songs in the show very much, but my part had hardly enough of them, although it had plenty of opportunities for comedians to compare me with elephants and heavyweight boxers.

I got out of bed and went to the washbasin to get a drink of water. It tasted warm and unpleasant and barely quenched my thirst. It didn't seem possible that anything would ever again be sweet and cool and refreshing. Of course I had known heat and humidity in Washington summers, but then I had not had to spend hours a day dancing and singing, and I was not battered with noise and light when I wanted to relax.

Perhaps I had at last dropped off to sleep and was dreaming, for something gold was gleaming and it was not the watch on the dressing table. I was back in the dining room at my home in Washington, and I recognized it as it was about a year and a half before I came

32

to New York. It was late on a Saturday night, and my grandparents were again visiting the family.

The thing that was gleaming was a five-dollar gold piece on the table. It caught the light from the lamps and seemed to bask in its shining glory. I was speaking to my mother, who sat at one side of the table sewing; the material lay on the table before her, beside her workbasket and scissors.

"That's the third this year, Mom," I said. "I wish you'd been there to see me."

"I hardly need to, Kathryn," she said with a chuckle, "I've heard you often enough upstairs practicing."

"What's that?" Granny Hanby asked. She was sitting at right angles to my mother and was occupied with some very intricate embroidery. Her hair was a little thinner now, and her eyeglasses were stronger, but the straightness of her back had not changed.

"Kathryn's Charleston," answered Mother. "You've never seen it, have you? We should get Kathryn to demonstrate for you."

Granny's mouth tightened a little. "I'm not sure I want to see it, Charlotte," she said.

Ignoring this, Mother went on. "This is the third gold piece she's won this year at the Keith Theatre."

"So that's how you won it," Granny said, looking at the gold coin with suspicion.

I hastened to put myself right with Granny, whose opinion meant a lot to me. "Not entirely, Granny—I only finish up with the Charleston. The main part of my act is songs, and then at the end I signal to the band leader, and off we go! The audience loves it," I added, not at all sure that Granny was won over.

"She worked hard at it upstairs in her bedroom for weeks," my mother added. "I used to wonder if the ceilings would stand all that pounding and jumping!"

Laughing, I asked Mother if I could have some milk and cookies because performing had made me hungry. There was an ominous silence in the dining room while I went to bring the food to the table. I wondered whether this was the time to break the news I had, and decided it would be better to wait a little.

Luckily Father and Grandpa came in at that moment from their evening walk to Father's lodge. Father saw the gold piece on the table and said, "So you've won another fortune, Kathryn? We'll soon have to have a safe in the house for all this gold."

Grandpa Hanby picked it up. "Must be quite an audience at these amateur nights if they can afford to give away these things, eh? Who judges the contest, Kathryn?"

"They do it by seeing which person gets most applause, Grandpa," I told him, "and my Charleston always seems to please them, so———"

"So you do the Charleston as well, eh? Well, it doesn't seem a very graceful dance from what I've heard, but I suppose there's no harm in it," he said, looking at Granny's pursed mouth.

Granny said nothing, but seemed absorbed in a particularly difficult stitch in her needlework.

The talk passed to other topics as Father and Grandpa sat down in chairs near the window. They would chat now in a relaxed way until it was time to go to bed. I took my empty milk glass out to the kitchen, and came back to my mother's side.

"Mother," I said softly, "the manager at the theater spoke to me tonight, just as I was leaving, and he said he was thinking of offering me a week's engagement because I'd won so many Saturday night contests. He said I could probably go on the bill with a comedian in March."

Mother put down her sewing. "Kathryn, I know it means a lot to you, but don't be too hasty. Ask your father what he thinks."

This was what I had been dreading, but I couldn't stop now; Father had already heard a few words of the conversation and had turned to me. "What was that about a comedian, Kathryn?" he asked.

"Father, the manager at the theater says that he will probably give me a week's engagement later in the season and——"

"Kathryn, I think we had better stop this before it goes any further and upsets you more. You simply cannot go on that stage for a week while you are still at school."

"Well, Father," I said, "he also said that if he couldn't

arrange it this season, I might be able to do it next season——"

"By that time, Kathryn, you'll be in nursing school
and things may be very different."

I suddenly saw red before my eyes and forgot myself.

"You mean, you hope I will have forgotten all about
singing, don't you? Well, I won't!" My voice became
very high-pitched.

"Kathryn!" My mother was upset. Granny put down
her embroidery and looked at me so severely that her
face seemed carved of stone. "You know that is no way
to speak to us——" but I interrupted her.

"Oh, why must you spoil my big chance? If I were to
go on for a week, someone from New York might see
me and then I'd go on Broadway——"

Granny's dry voice rose above mine. "And someone
from New York might not see you and you'd be more
disappointed than ever. Kathryn, we know what's best
for you."

I was sobbing now. "Oh, no, you don't, you don't,
Granny. I want to sing, I want to go on the stage, I
don't want to go to nursing school!"

"Besides," said Granny, raising her voice above mine
and ignoring my rudeness, "I don't want any granddaughter of mine laughed at for shaking her legs on the
stage doing that silly dance."

"Granny, I won't do the Charleston always. I want to
sing, but you've got to do something else so that people
will notice you."

This didn't placate Granny. "And what else will you have to do after that so that you'll keep on being noticed? And what sort of life will you lead with those stage people? They seem to spend their lives drinking and smoking and getting divorced. You have been brought up to fear God and know what is right——"

"I can still do that and be on the stage, can't I?" My voice had risen still higher. "I don't have to get like some others."

"The temptations are there, Kathryn, and you are too young to be exposed to them."

My mother's gentle voice contrasted with Granny's severity.

"Kathryn, you'll still be able to sing when you are a nurse. There are always concerts in hospitals and you can still belong to the St. Pat's Players and the church choir."

"It isn't the same, it isn't the same!" I laid my head on my arms on the table and sobbed. I felt the grown-ups' uneasiness. I don't think they, any more than I, wanted this scene. But the seeds of the quarrel had already been sown.

I lifted my head and looked through sore eyes at my mother.

"Mom, don't you see it isn't the same? I don't want to be an amateur appearing in shows that aren't properly rehearsed and have to play with people who are in them because if they were left out their feelings might be hurt. I want to be a professional, I want to work at my singing. I want to give my whole life to it. I know I can do it!"

Grandpa Hanby rose from his chair, came over to me and put his hand on my shoulder. "Kathryn Elizabeth," he said, "there are many, many girls who feel as sure of themselves as you do and who try to go on the stage. Then they find it too hard for them, they fall into bad company, and they have to come back home, often to hide their disgrace. We don't want this to happen to you."

"But, Grandpa," I said, looking up at his white hair and wishing he would smile, "those girls didn't have talent and they weren't interested in anything but the glamour of the stage. I know I can sing. Look!" I pointed to the gold coin.

"Yes, Kathryn, I know, but that was only against other amateurs. What about competition with other professionals?" He walked to the window and stood with his back to the curtains.

"And Kathryn," said my father's voice, "don't forget that you—well, you have a handicap——"

"You mean I'm fat, don't you? Why don't you say what you mean? That's twice——"

"Kathryn, that's enough!" came sharply from my grandmother, but I couldn't stop. It seemed to me as if I was putting up a last resistance against forces which were trying to push me into the oblivion of nursing school. I didn't dream that there could ever be a second chance; if I didn't fight now, I would never sing on the stage, never be happy in my whole life.

"Father, I know I'm fat and I know I wear glasses and my hair is straight, but I can sing!"

"We should never have encouraged her," said Granny in a low voice, shaking her head at my mother, "never have encouraged her."

I went on passionately. "People don't want to look at me, they want to hear my voice. You don't understand, you don't understand!"

"Stop shouting, Kathryn," said my father sharply. He got up and came to my mother's side. "Now listen and let's stop this before you say anything else to hurt us all. We know better than you because we've lived longer and we know that the stage is no place for a young girl. Kathryn, we want you to be happy and lead a normal life——"

"A normal life!" All my rancor and bitterness came out now, and nothing would stop me. "What sort of normal life can I lead? When do I ever get taken out on dates like other girls? I never get a date, never! In school they laugh at me——" A great gust of self-pity took hold of me and I sobbed as if my heart would break.

"Well, then, what would they do on the stage?" said Father.

This threw me into further frenzy. Why couldn't they understand that it was different, quite different when I sang? Why was my family so stupid? I began to get quite hysterical, and my breath came in long dry gasps. They were all against me, everybody was against me—even the people I loved. I felt Father's hand on my shoulder shaking me hard. I went on sobbing.

"Be quiet, Kathryn, be quiet." I couldn't stop. Then I felt a stinging blow on the side of my face and I looked at father's upraised arm. The sobs slowly came to a halt and I saw clearly again. Mother was quietly weeping, and Granny held her hand across the table. There were no other sounds and the house seemed suddenly eerily silent. Father put his hand on Mother's shoulder and spoke gently to her.

"Don't cry, Charlotte, don't cry. Do you think you could go in the kitchen and make us all some coffee? Then we'll quietly settle this once for all."

My mother and grandmother rose from the table, my mother drying her eyes with a handkerchief as they went out. Grandpa sat down in the chair by the window, and Father passed a hand over his brow. His face looked more tired than I had ever seen it, and I wondered if he were ill. The atmosphere slowly lost its electric intensity; I sat sniffling, a bundle of tearful misery.

"Get out your handkerchief, Kathryn," said Father severely.

I wiped my eyes and contemplated the hopelessness of my position. It was no use; they were all stronger than I was, and my life was to be martyred to satisfy their wishes. I saw it all clearly: I saw myself telling the manager of the theater that I could not accept the engagement because my parents didn't want me to go on the stage. I could see myself in a white uniform, working unnoticed for many years and at last dying, unknown, unmarried and unsung. Adolescent miseries include no compromises—everything is either rosy or jet black, and my future was going to be the blackest possible.

Mother carried a tray into the room and served coffee in silence broken only by those colorless remarks that people make when they want to bring things back to normal. Father took a few sips from his cup, and then put it down with a sharp clink into the saucer.

"Now, Kathryn," he said, firmly but kindly, "let's get this straight. We love you, and it's because we love you that we're being so cruel, as you think, now. We love to hear you sing, and we thank God that He gave you such a lovely voice, but we don't want you to suffer the unnecessary competition of a stage career. We think of you as a person, not as a singer, and we want to protect you from misery and degradation. Is that clear? We think that after a little time you'll find yourself so absorbed in being a nurse that you'll forget all about this ambition. And you'll always be able to sing for us, you know. Now then, kiss your mother and apologize for all the hurtful things you said."

I did so, meek as a lamb. My mother held my hand and said, "It won't be as bad as you think, Kathryn."

My grandmother held out her arms to me. "Kathryn, pray to God tonight for strength and thank Him that you have such thoughtful parents who love you. You will thank us in later years that we saved your soul from peril." I wept a little as she kissed my cheek.

Grandpa Hanby kissed me too. "Good night, little Kathryn. You can always sing to me, you know."

I went to kiss my father good night. He held me close and whispered, "I'm sorry I slapped you, Kathryn. Say a prayer for me too."

I went off upstairs to bed, feeling that my life was shattered.

It was curious, I thought as I looked up at the ceiling, that they had warned me of the wrong things. A screaming siren had brought me to full wakefulness and I was back in the reality of humid air and an aching head. I suppose it was because they were entirely ignorant of the stage except from hearsay, for no member of the family had ever become a professional performer. They had warned me of immorality, but far from being tempted by unhealthy company, I was miserable because I had no company at all; it was loneliness, not sin, which beset me. They had told me my weight, then about 190 pounds, would be a handicap to my career, whereas I now acknowledged, to my dismay, that it had actually gotten me this part in "Honeymoon Lane."

I wearily got up from the bed and got my watch from the dressing table. One-thirty. My legs ached as I stood in the middle of the room. I walked to the window and looked out through the screen. The red sign must have been below me and to my left, but I couldn't lean out and see what it advertised. I looked at the black buildings of New York; some were lit up inside so that they looked like the pumpkins with candles inside them we always made on Hallowe'en. I thought of the people who must be asleep at this moment: Mother and Father and Helene at home, Granny and Grandpa in Maryland, the other members of the cast of "Honeymoon Lane" in hotels like this one; Phyllis, who might be asleep, but who might also be on night duty, sitting at a desk in a quiet ward in Washington, watching the irregular shapes of sleeping patients.

Phyllis and I had become great friends as soon as I went to nursing school. She was a born nurse; rather plump and short, with sensitive, capable hands and a lovely clear complexion. She was always cheerful, quick and efficient. She loved her job and was scrupulous both in obeying orders and in learning theory for the classroom sessions. I was neither, for I was always daydreaming about singing in big productions on Broadway; no matter how hard I tried, visions of applauding audiences would always come between me and the intricate drawings of some part of the human anatomy I was supposed to be studying. In spite of Phyllis' great love for nursing, she understood my problem and sympathized with it; I often confided to her how I felt about going on the stage.

One day we were making beds in an empty ward together. As usual, her side of the bed was made with a precision like that of a mathematical equation, while on my side, in spite of all my efforts, bits of sheet seemed to stick out and creases would not come smooth. Phyllis herself looked as neat as the corner tuck she made in the sheet, while my uniform seemed crumpled, the hem felt too long, the sleeves too tight. I began to tell Phyllis how discouraged I was that I couldn't sink myself into learning how to be a nurse and couldn't forget the stage. She suddenly put down the blanket we were folding.

"Kate, why don't you give up nursing?" she asked.

"I wish I could," I answered, "but my parents would be so mad at me if I did."

"They'll be madder still if you go on feeling miserable, making a mess of things and flunking your exams."

"I suppose so. But there'll be another fuss about it if I tell them I'm going to give it up. And I haven't got an engagement in sight in any theater and I don't know if I'd ever get one."

"Look, Kate," said Phyllis, with her usual practicality. "You told me once that the booking office wanted to give you a week's engagement, right? And you have got some money saved, haven't you? Why don't you go and see the manager again? He was very enthusiastic about you a year ago, and he might let you sing on a couple of Saturday nights before giving you a week on the bill. While you're waiting you could learn a lot more new songs, practice the Charleston and live on your savings. Your mother wouldn't expect you to pay for your keep, would she? And after you'd talked to the manager, you could tell your parents that you've decided to give up nursing in order to have some chance of succeeding on the stage."

"Oh, I don't know, Phyllis. I don't want there to be another row and there isn't much chance——"

"Kate Smith," said Phyllis in the voice she has used ever since with great success on recalcitrant patients, "do you believe you can sing well enough to earn your living at it?"

"Yes," I said, for deep down I believed it.

"Then go ahead and do it. You know very well that if you want anything badly enough you can get it."

Nevertheless, it was not for some months that I actually gave up nursing. I performed at a few Saturday amateur nights and won some more five-dollar gold pieces, and finally quit nursing school when the manager gave me a definite engagement for a week on a bill which was to include Eddie Dowling as the star performer.

I left the window and brought my watch back with me to the bedside table. I sat down on the edge of the bed and stared at the carpet, which was dingy and, in the daytime, discernibly beige. But now only the patches where things had been spilled showed up. It didn't look much like the carpets I was used to at home, and it didn't look much like the carpet in the manager's office in that Washington theater, either.

The whole of that week during which I was performing for the first time as a professional I was praying for a miracle. There was a definite "on approval" atmosphere at home; I knew that if I didn't get other engagements I should have to swallow my pride, and turn to some other job which wouldn't be as rewarding as nursing.

I didn't know it, but my prayers were answered when a messenger came after the last performance of the week to the dressing room I shared with all the other women performers and asked me to go to the manager's office as soon as I was dressed. I hoped that it would be an offer of another week—that would be enough to justify me to my parents and grandparents, to stop them from saying "I told you so" when I failed.

When I entered the manager's office I stepped onto a carpet, an unaccustomed feeling after the bare boards of the stage and our communal dressing room. Sitting beside the desk in a leather armchair was a fat man dressed in evening clothes and wearing a white silk scarf; he was smoking a cigar, and did not rise when I came in. The manager said, "Oh, here you are, Kate—this is Mr. Erlanger, Abe Erlanger. This is Kate Smith, Mr. Erlanger." He sat down at his desk and looked at us throughout the rest of the conversation.

"Sit down, Kate," said Mr. Erlanger, flicking his cigar ash into an ashtray on the desk. I found a straight office chair against the wall and sat in that. "Enjoyed your act very much, Kate," went on Mr. Erlanger. "That's some voice you've got there. How long've you been taking lessons?"

I could barely find my voice to say that I had never

taken lessons. "I sing by ear—I can't read music," I told him.

His eyebrows lifted on his crinkled forehead, which seemed very high because he was getting bald. "How long d' you take to learn a song, then?" he asked.

"Oh, I can usually repeat it after hearing it once, but of course I have to polish it up and sing it lots of times to get it the way I want it. I guess I'm lucky—I have perfect pitch," I answered.

"Look here, Kate," he said, seeming not to have heard my answer and glancing at his watch, "I think you'd be good on Broadway. I'm producing a new show called 'Honeymoon Lane' and there's a part in it for you— Tiny Little. Kind of a song and dance part. You'll do your Charleston and sing a few numbers."

"Oh, Mr. Erlanger," I began, but I couldn't speak for surprise and I certainly hadn't noticed the implications of the name Tiny Little.

"Well, look, I'm in a hurry, Kate, so I'll just give you a check now, and mail the contract to you later, okay? We're gonna open in New York in September, but there'll be several weeks somewhere else first. By the way, how old're you?"

"I'm nearly seventeen, Mr. Erlanger," I said.

He was signing a check on the edge of the desk and getting up to leave at the same time. "Best to start young," he said. "Here y'are. See you on Broadway in September, Kate." With a hurried good-by he was gone, leaving only the smell of his very good cigar in the

47

room. I sat there, holding the check stupidly, unable to believe it. The manager roused me by saying, "Congratulations, Kate, it's a great break."

As soon as I took the news home, opposition to my going on the stage was at an end. My mother, whom I always suspected of sympathy with my ambitions from the start, although she had not wanted to oppose my father, began to make preparations for me, helping me buy my clothes and providing me with new suitcases. She did not doubt that I would be traveling frequently in my new life and she realized the importance of a good set of luggage to take heavy wear—and also to look handsome in hotel lobbies. My father said, "Kathryn, it's obvious that this is what you want, and I admire you for having stuck it out. You have my blessing."

Granny and Grandpa Hanby were pleased, but not rapturous. They came from an older generation and could not ever be expected to approve entirely. I asked them if they would come and see me on Broadway when I was established. "I don't know about that," replied Granny Hanby. "We'll have to see how it all turns out."

The next few weeks were a flurry of letters to and from the production office in New York. I got copies of my contract, instructions on where and when I was to report for rehearsals, copies of my script and the music. When I examined my part, I realized that Mr. Erlanger's interest in me was not solely confined to my voice, as I had hoped. I was to be a buffoon, but my delight at having been discovered swept all doubts aside as I went on with my preparations. Think of it! I kept saying to myself: Broadway, New York, success, footlights, music, people in glamorous evening dress, rave reviews, great songs, wave after wave of applause.

And here it was: a poor hotel room because my salary was not as high as my aspirations, homesickness, exhaustion after the continual grueling rehearsals, and loneliness. I swung my legs up on the bed and leaned back on the pillow. I looked at my watch: 2:15. Would sleep never come? Would I lie here going over and over what had brought me here until it was time to get up and go to rehearsal again? I groaned. Perhaps if I thought of something pleasant it might relax me . . .

I remembered my mother's sweet face as together we finished packing my valises in my bedroom on the night before I left for New York. We had been chatting happily about what I would do in New York, when she suddenly stopped, put down the dress she was folding and faced me squarely.

"Kathryn," she said, "I wish I could go with you. It breaks my heart to think of your going off alone like this. I'd be going too if it weren't for Helene and your father. But just remember this: if ever you are unhappy, you have a home to come back to. Don't hesitate to leave it all and come here. I'll never reproach you for one moment if you can't take it."

She pulled me close against her and we both wept a little. Then we finished the packing and went downstairs for my last meal at home.

My heavy eyelids drooped and I finally began to doze. The comforting thought was there. My pride would not let me turn back, but it was enough to know I would be welcome if I did. The last thing I saw was the red light going out; I fell asleep before it flashed on again.

Three

I T W A S four years before Granny and Grandpa Hanby were able to come to New York to see me on the stage. I think it took them as long as that not only because New York was further than they were accustomed to traveling but because they wanted to be sure that I was not going to change my mind and come back home.

I was outwardly quite a different person at twenty-one from the unhappy girl who had suffered from homesickness in the summer of 1926. I was now an established musical comedy actress with a wide repertory of songs and many varied styles of singing them. I soon had my own apartment in New York and could command quite a luxurious salary; I made regular trips home to Washington every weekend, very often taking small gifts for my family. "Honeymoon Lane" had been a great success. The critics, with a few witticisms about my weight, had hailed me as a promising newcomer and the public followed them into the theater. After a year on Broadway, the show went on the road for another year and I enjoyed the intoxicating experience of becoming a trouper.

When "Honeymoon Lane" finally closed at the beginning of 1929, I was offered the part of the colored Mammy in the touring company of "Hit the Deck." For the next six months I shook the rafters in theaters all over the United States with "Hallelujah!" When we came back to New York, I was given a contract to appear at the beginning of 1930 in a new musical comedy, "Flying High." I was to sing a number of songs in the show, but also act as stooge for the comedians because of my size.

But my success had not brought with it the happiness I had anticipated. The public thought of me first as a fat girl who good-naturedly endured the very funny remarks of clowns, and only second as a singer. A number of young men about town used to make bets with each other about how much I ate at a sitting; then one would come around after the show and invite me to supper at Lindy's or one of the other Broadway restaurants. Throughout the meal he would press food on me in an embarrassing manner, and usually people at nearby tables would begin to snicker. After a few experiments of this sort, I refused all such invitations.

I didn't find much social life within the company of "Flying High," either. After the show groups of people in the cast would go out to eat together or to dine and dance at a night club, but I was never asked to join them. I didn't smoke or drink and got tired about midnight, so it was considered I would be a drag on the company around a night-club table.

Only a few weeks after "Flying High" opened, I received a telegram in the middle of the afternoon at my apartment. It was from our family doctor in Washington, asking me to come home right away; my father was very ill. He had always looked tired, and we knew that this was caused by diabetes. Apparently the illness had taken a turn for the worse.

What could I do? I would have to get the next train out of New York and I would miss the show, perhaps for a few days. I did not imagine there would be any difficulty about it; I certainly could not sing when my father was ill and might be dying.

I telephoned George White, the producer of the show, and told him I wanted to leave New York at once. His dry voice over the wire didn't sound very friendly.

"Now, wait a minute, Kate, don't be so hasty. We've got a show to consider, ya know. People always get so excited about a little illness and start sending telegrams. It's probably not as bad as your mother thinks——"

I broke in on him. "But Mr. White, the doctor sent the telegram."

"Ah, Kate, these doctors, they take everything so seriously."

"But my father has diabetes, and this might be the last time I'd see him."

"Now let's not be dramatic about this. Have you thought what would happen to the show if you didn't go on tonight?" he said sharply.

"No, I haven't——"

"Obviously. Well, we wouldn't be able to put the show on because we couldn't get an understudy ready in time, and we'd lose all that money."

"Mr. White, my father's probably dying and I have to——"

"You have a contract with me Kate, and you can't break it. And what's more, if you didn't turn up tonight, I'd hold you personally responsible for the loss. You'd have to pay me and the company for all the seat money we'd have to give back, the rent on the theater, the wages of the stage staff——"

"But Mr. White, I'd never have enough money——"

"Well, then, we'd attach your salary until you paid it. You've got to realize just how serious it is not to fulfill your contract, no matter who's supposed to be dying. You can go home right after the show." There was an abrupt click at the other end of the line.

I was appalled, not so much by Mr. White's inhumanity, but by the thought that I could ever be held responsible for so great a debt. I was cowed into putting all thoughts of going home aside, and just prayed that my father was not as ill as I feared. I did not know, for I had hitherto little experience of this sort, that Mr. White's threats would not stand up in a court, and I had no friends in the company of "Flying High" to advise me.

As soon as the curtain came down, I was off the stage and in my dressing-room changing to street clothes for the dash to Pennsylvania Station. I removed my make-up on the train, for I hadn't time before I left the Apollo Theatre. The journey was such misery that I afterward forgot the details of it. I sent up prayer after prayer for my father, and urged the train along as fast as it would go.

When I got to Union Station in Washington, I ran from the train and almost screamed for a taxi. But my haste was of no use. When I got to our house, the taxi pulled up behind an undertaker's car.

After the funeral, I went back to New York full of bitterness. Whenever I saw George White backstage after that I looked straight through him and refused to acknowledge him. I didn't care if he threw me out of "Flying High." The theater must be a rotten place, I felt, if men like him flourished in it. From that day onward, I vowed, whenever my family wanted me, I would give up everything to go to them, no matter what. "The show must go on" was meaningless to me.

After my father's funeral, I tried to bring my mother back to New York to live with me permanently, but she still had my sister to look after and was only able to come for a few days at a time.

My part in "Flying High" was becoming increasingly painful for me. The digs at my size were doubly upsetting in my private grief. I reluctantly began to think that I was not cut out for show business after all—at least, not this kind of show business. I could not separate myself off stage from myself on stage, as so many actors can. When I went on to sing or to play stooge to the leading comedian, I did not leave the dull burden of my unhappiness in the dressing room, but carried it right on with me so that the comedian's remarks only added to it. Conversely, when I went home to my apartment, the jokes and the derisive laughter were still ringing in my ears and no amount of quiet conversation with Mother when she was there could drown them out.

Perhaps it was my mother who suggested to Granny and Grandpa that a visit from them, long overdue in any case, might cheer me up at this point. They wrote a letter telling me that they were going to come to New York for a day and a night; they asked me to reserve a hotel room and two good seats for "Flying High." They explained that their eyes were not as good as they used to be and they wanted to be close to the stage to see their Kathryn Elizabeth clearly.

Delighted as I was to see them, their arrival brought

with it misgivings that only added to my discomfort
about my part in "Flying High." As we chatted and
laughed on our way out of the railroad station that
morning—walking a little aimlessly because we were
more interested in each other than in where we were
going—I realized that they had very different ideas
about my success from those of a Broadway audience.
Granny and Grandpa had obviously been told their
granddaughter was very funny in this show, but their
idea of what was amusing stemmed from their simplicity
and their God-fearing country life in Maryland.

As I showed them the sights with pride—for I was
beginning then to acquire that affection for New York
which has since made me never want to live anywhere
else—my mind was trying to answer the question: what
can I do? Is there any way in which I can make my part
seem less offensive just for one night? I got more and
more nervous as the day progressed, until the palms
of my hands were greasy with perspiration. Finally I
steered Granny and Grandpa back to their hotel, and
told them to eat some dinner. I explained that I never
ate anything myself before a show, but would cook up
something in my apartment afterward while we all
talked over the performance. My smile concealed a
great dread about that meal.

I fled to the Apollo Theatre, and sat in my dressing
room for a few moments to calm myself. It was still
very early, but from the sounds of whistling down the
corridor I could tell that one of the comedians was in his

room. He was a very conscientious actor, never late, and meticulous in rehearsing and practicing. If he had not been one of my chief tormentors I think I would have admired the way he did his job very much.

I knocked at the door of his dressing room.

"May I come in?" I asked.

"Okay," he said, "but look out for the——"

It was too late. I had opened the door and tripped over a basket which stood in the way. A chair stopped me from actually falling; I clung to its back and caught my breath for a moment. I noticed that the comedian was leaning against his dressing table flinching away from me.

"Phew!" he said. "Thank Heaven you didn't fall on me. They'd have had to scrape me up with a palette knife."

That convinced me that the errand I had come on was a useless one, but I thought I would at least try.

"Look," I began, "I—may I sit down?"

"Sure," he said. "The chairs are strong—I hope."

I sat there trembling with nervousness. "I want to ask you a favor. It means a lot to me. My grandparents are watching the show tonight and I wish you'd just go easy on the ad-libs. I don't mind the part itself, but your ad-libs—well, they aren't necessary and they do sort of make me look more silly than ever."

He stood by his mirror laughing soundlessly for a moment. Then he sat down facing me, his face hard and unkind, and said, "Kate, this is show business. You're a stooge and I'm there to get laughs out of you. If I stick to the script, sure, I get laughs, but when I feel the audience with me, why should I stop there? This show's a hit already, but it's got to go on being a hit, and one way we can make sure of that is to make 'em laugh more and more."

"But, look, I'm only asking for one night. My grandparents weren't out there yesterday and they won't be there tomorrow, they're just there tonight. I don't care what you do any other time, but just for tonight . . ."

He got up and went to open the door for me. "Kate, if Al Smith and Mayor Walker like the show the way it is, what do I care for your grandparents? What did you get into show business for if you can't take it?"

I went out miserably into the corridor, now full of actors chatting to each other as they went to their dressing rooms. The leading man came to the door behind me and called to another of the comedians, "Hey, Joe, Kate here wants us to cut out the ad-libs tonight. Sure we will, huh?" The other man winked back and they both burst into derisive laughter that followed me into my dressing room, where I made up with my heart pumping nervously and my hands trembling.

As soon as I came on stage it started. "Well, here comes a little lady sitting on top of the world—and boy, nothing else would bear that weight!" It was a terrible joke, but it got a laugh and applause. While I stood there smiling, my eyes searched the front seats for Granny and Grandpa. There they were, but they weren't applauding and their faces were set, even a little puzzled. I hoped they could see I was looking at them, giving them a little secret smile.

The jokes got worse and there were more of them as the show progressed. I could see Granny and Grandpa becoming more and more puzzled and upset. My eyes kept straying to them throughout the time I was on stage, and they never laughed or applauded. Their faces became a little more relaxed when I sang, but a cloud settled on them when the comedians began again. It seemed to me that never had the ad-libs been more numerous and never in more deplorable taste. I watched Grandpa's face grow dark with anger, and I was afraid that he was going to stand up in the audience and shout at the comedian from there.

Somehow the show ground through to its end. The applause was tumultuous that night and we took many curtain calls. As I stood there in the line I watched Granny and Grandpa walk from their seats to the exit; I had told them to come back to my dressing room and I wondered whether my grandmother's set lips would ever smile at me again.

They certainly didn't there. I was putting cream on my face when there was a knock at the door and one of the call-boys said, "Here's your visitors, Miss Smith." Granny and Grandpa walked in, Grandpa holding his hat stiffly in one hand. They said nothing. In a broken voice I asked them to sit down, and told them I wouldn't be long getting dressed. They still said nothing; Grandpa sat with his hat on one knee and Granny perched in her chair without touching the back. They both eyed the mirror, the lights, the sticks of make-up, the dresses hung in the open closet, as if they were dirty and untouchable. I took my shower and dressed in an atmosphere which was as oppressive as the dark sky before a thunderstorm.

It was not until we were back at my apartment and I was fixing my supper that they finally spoke. I put the coffee pot on the table and sat down; some stew was warming in a pan on the kitchen stove and I was waiting for it to be ready. Granny, who was sitting in a straight chair watching me, said in an unexpectedly gentle voice, "Kathryn Elizabeth, this is no life for you. Why don't you forget all about the stage and that . . . that terrible play and come home with us?"

"Granny," I began, "you don't understand. I can't just quit like that——"

"And you can't go on being insulted like that, either," broke in my grandfather's voice. He got up from the easy chair where he had been sitting without real comfort and walked to the window. As he turned to me I noticed that he was wearing his vest and the watch on its chain. "Kathryn, have you no more respect for yourself than to allow yourself to be used as a butt for such cheap, nasty remarks, evening after evening? We thought you were supposed to be funny in this play, but if that is humor, then it doesn't amuse either your grandmother or myself."

I got up to get the stew from the kitchen, but when I brought it back, it didn't seem so appetizing after all. I poured the coffee.

Granny spoke as she stirred her coffee. "When you wanted to go on the stage, Kathryn, we thought you were going to be a singer, and although we didn't really approve of the stage as a place for a young girl, we could see that if you were so eager to sing, you had to do it. But this isn't what we expected."

"Granny, Grandpa, let me tell you I don't like it either. It's been getting worse and worse ever since 'Flying High' began, and I've been thinking I ought to get out of it."

"Then why don't you?" said Grandpa, his tall figure silhouetted against the window in the lamp-light.

"Because of my contract. You see, I have to stay with the show at least until it closes in New York and because it's a hit, it may run for a long time."

Granny put her coffee cup on the table. "I don't understand these city folks. That's a hit, is it? I wonder how many of them there go to church on Sunday and pray to be forgiven for laughing at a poor girl just because she's a bit fatter than they are?"

"I go to church every Sunday," I said to Granny, hoping to placate her.

"Well, then, Kathryn," said Grandpa, "I hope when

this contract runs out, you'll come home and forget all about the stage. I only pray that the play won't run very long so that you are not more damaged by it than you are now."

"You can't wish it any more than I do," I said, very near to tears. Grandpa came over to me and put his strong arms around my shoulders.

"Kathryn, since your father died I feel I have a double responsibility for you, even though you're a grown woman now. When you come home, we'll see if we can find something for you to do, but first of all you'll need a good long vacation to forget all about this singing."

I sat up very straight. "Grandpa, you don't understand—I don't want to give up singing, I only want to give up musical comedy."

Granny's face lost the smile that had softened it at last. "But, Kathryn, haven't you learned your lesson yet?" she said, almost irritably.

Grandpa had moved a step away from me, and I looked from Granny to him as I answered, "Yes, I have learned my lesson. I've learned that I tried to do things too quickly—I should never have taken that offer when I was seventeen, but waited for something more suited to me. But I still love singing."

They both sighed. Grandpa sat down in the armchair again.

Granny patted her gray hair in its neat little bun at the back of her head. "I don't know what to think about you, Kathryn. You've been through all this, and you admit you don't like it, but yet you still want to go on singing. You're too difficult for me to understand.

"Dear Granny," I put my hand out to her over the table. "I don't know yet how I'll find a way to sing without having to be in musical comedy, but I feel sure I will. Maybe I'll go home and take lots of singing lessons and then sing at concerts; maybe I'll even try opera. I don't know, but I do know I must go on singing. God tells me," I added softly to Granny.

"I thank Him for your faith, at least," she answered. Grandpa sat silent. Granny poured us all more coffee.

"You know, I might even be able to sing on this new wireless system," I ventured, to ease the atmosphere.

"No, no," said Grandpa, shaking his head, "that's being foolish, Kathryn. That thing's just a novelty—they'll have forgotten all about it in a year or two."

My one attempt at lightening the atmosphere had not been successful and I made no others. Gloom settled on us until Granny and Grandpa left, disappointed that I would not give up my desire to sing professionally.

My grandparents' disgust at "Flying High" seemed to add weight to the cross I already had to bear. Word had got around the company that I had asked the comedian to go slow on the ad-libs that night and from then on my life was hardly worth living in the theater, on or off stage. When my mother was visiting me in New York, I could go home and tell her about my troubles, but when I was alone, I often gave way to tears. In addition, although I had told Granny and Grandpa with conviction in my voice that there were other ways of earning my living by singing, it didn't seem as if any of them were going to open to me. On the other hand, I couldn't reconcile myself to going back to Washington and singing at amateur concerts again. It seemed there was no way out.

However, I did find the courage to tell the producers of "Flying High" that I would leave the cast when the show ended in New York and that I would not be going on the road with it. This meant that I was giving myself a definite date by which to decide on my future.

One evening a couple of months after my grandparents came to New York, I was removing my make-up in my dressing room after the show, staring at my face in the mirror. It was gray with worry and there was no sparkle in the eyes. A few whisps of damp straight hair clung to the forehead where the cream had caught them and taken out the artificial curl. It was a forlorn face. A knock sounded on the door.

"Can I come in, Miss Smith? A man wants to see you and he's sent his card," said the voice of a call-boy.

I went to the door in my make-up wrapper and took the card from the boy. If a man wanted to see me, it could only be one of those playboys hoping to see how many steaks I could eat; there was no man who could be the slightest bit interested in me. I read the card on which was printed: "Ted Collins, Recording Manager, Columbia Phonograph Company."

"I don't know any man named Collins," I told the boy. "I don't want to see him."

"Look on the other side," said the boy. I thought this Mr. Collins must have tipped him pretty well.

The other side of the card bore two scrawled words: "Strictly business," and was signed with the initials, "T.C."

"Go on, Miss Smith," urged the boy, when I had finished reading the card. "He's all right."

"All right," I said with a sigh. "Tell him I'll see him in ten minutes when I'm dressed." I closed the door, looked at the card again, tore it up quickly and threw it into the trash basket along with the bits of cotton and candy-bar wrappers.

I was dressed and putting on my lipstick at the mirror when the second knock sounded on my door. I called "Come in!" and continued sitting at the mirror, so that I saw my visitor first in reflection. He was a young man of about middle height with black hair and a round, pugnacious face. This much I grasped from one look at him in the mirror.

"Good evening, Miss Smith," he said politely. His voice was very pleasing, well modulated and had a slight Irishness in it. "I enjoyed your singing very much this evening and I just wanted to ask you——"

"Thanks very much, Mr. Collins," I said wearily,

completely misunderstanding his intentions, "but I always eat supper at home after the show." I expected him to back out with an apology after this. Instead, he put his brown hat on the chest of drawers and smiled at me.

"Miss Smith, I said I enjoyed your singing this evening, and it's about that that I want to talk to you. May I sit down?"

Something in the emphasis on the word "singing" caught my attention. For the first time I turned from the mirror and looked at my visitor face to face. I motioned him to a chair and looked at him with more interest than any human being had aroused in me for a long time. He had frank, confident brown eyes.

"Miss Smith, I'm recording manager for the Columbia Phonograph Company. Have you ever had your voice recorded?"

"No, I haven't," I answered.

"Would you like to? I sat out front tonight listening to your singing and I felt what a shame it was that only the people in that theater could hear your lovely voice. I thought that if I could get it on a record, many more people would enjoy it as I did."

"Well, now, Mr. Collins, I never thought of it. What would I have to do?"

"You'd just come over to the Columbia Phonograph Company's studios, and sing as you sang tonight. I think it would probably be even nicer because you'd be singing for only a few people—the recording engineers and myself—and it would be like singing at home."

"It certainly sounds interesting, Mr. Collins, but what's the trick in it? Do I have to pay you for recording my voice?"

"Oh, no, Miss Smith," he answered. "Since I've asked *you* to do the recording, there'll be something in it for you—especially if the records sell, as I'm sure they will. Now, what about it? Can I make a date for you to come over to the studios?"

"Well, yes, I guess you can. I wasn't figuring on doing anything in the afternoons for the next few days."

We arranged an afternoon appointment for the following week, and Mr. Collins wrote down the address and the time he wanted me there.

"Now, do I have to rehearse anything special for you, Mr. Collins?"

"No, no, Miss Smith, just come prepared to sing the songs you like best. There'll be a pianist there and he has the music for most popular songs. Okay? So long 'til next week," he said, picking up his hat and walking to the door. His back was very straight and his step had purpose in it.

I sat there for some time looking at the address and time on the piece of paper. Well, this was something new, I thought, but it wouldn't solve the basic problem. I thought very much more about that than I did about the Columbia Phonograph Company and Mr. Collins during the next few days.

He came to collect me at the reception desk when I arrived, slightly early, for my appointment. Before, I had merely noticed his bright eyes and rather boyish round face. Now I began to like them. When he took me into the recording studio, he introduced me to the few people there—the recording engineers and the pianist. I talked to the pianist about the song I wanted to sing and we ran over it together. Then I said I was ready.

"Don't you want to rehearse?" asked Mr. Collins.

"Well, I'm sure about my song, if everyone else is ready," I answered in all innocence. The recording engineers looked at each other. I began to wonder what I'd done wrong.

"In that case, we'll go ahead," said Mr. Collins, "but don't be surprised if we have to do it over and over again." I couldn't imagine why at the time. There's no second chance on the stage and I was trained to make the most of my first chance.

At a signal from Mr. Collins, I began to sing. In spite of the strangeness of the place, I found I was enjoying myself almost as much as I had when I sang to my family at home. I found myself smiling as we came to the end of the number. I looked at Mr. Collins. He seemed to be in a sort of trance, for his eyes were closed and he was keeping time with a pencil on the desk.

"Okay, boys," he said, coming awake. "Let's hear it through." I was very excited at the prospect of hearing my own voice for the first time. Like everyone else on such occasions, I didn't recognize it at first, particularly not among all the additional noises associated with recording in those days.

"That's me?" I asked. "Squeaking like that?" Everyone laughed, but Mr. Collins said, "It's not bad for the first time, Miss Smith. Let's try it again."

Toward the end of the song this time I was put off by a wrong note in the accompaniment and stopped singing. I blushed in confusion at having made a mess of things and apologized. I explained that I had heard a discordant note in the accompaniment; I felt rather badly for having blamed the pianist.

"No, that's all right, Miss Smith—we'd have heard it when we played it back anyway," said Mr. Collins. "But how could you hear it then?"

I blushed again. "I don't know, but I can hear a wrong note even in an orchestra. Takes the pleasure away lots of times!"

By the end of that afternoon, the recording engineers seemed satisfied and Mr. Collins' round face was smiling broadly. I found that I had enjoyed it all more than I had enjoyed anything for a long time and went to the theater for the evening show with a pleasant glow inside me.

A few weeks later Mr. Collins came again to the dressing room after the show, and told me that he had managed to place my first record with a few retail record dealers. Since it had sold quite a few copies, he wanted to ask me if I'd like to do another record for Columbia. When we had made arrangements for what he termed a recording session, he stood up, took his hat from the chest of drawers and said, "Now, Miss Smith,

I'd like to ask you the question you thought I wanted to ask you when I came here first. Would you like to come and eat some supper with me? And this time you know my intentions are only to talk about records with you."

We went, not to one of the big show business restaurants on Broadway, but to a small German one on Fourteenth Street; it was one of Mr. Collins' favorite places, but he knew, too, that I would not be intruded upon there. Throughout the meal we talked—or rather, he talked and I listened—about phonograph records; he seemed to know every record that had ever been made since Edison first got a sound out of the phonograph in 1877. He told me about the great future he foresaw for records; how everyone would one day have a phonograph in his home as naturally as he had chairs.

"There are only two companies now, Miss Smith—ours and the Victor outfit. But in a few years there'll be literally hundreds, all over the United States, and every sort of music you can imagine will be on records. Tell you something else—this radio thing's going to be big, too, really big."

"Wireless?" I said. "But my grandfather said it was only a novelty and would be forgotten in a couple of years."

"Couldn't be more wrong, unless I miss my guess—and I don't often do that."

As I went home in a taxi after dinner I felt excited by Mr. Collins' enthusiasm, but I reflected that, strangely enough, I hadn't learned very much more

about him as a person. I knew he was married, had a
little girl eight years old, and lived outside the city in
Rockaway Park. I wanted to know more about him. I
did not usually feel this about people I met in the course
of business, but Mr. Collins seemed to have more than a
purely business significance for me. Already his encouraging remarks about prospects in records, and his desire
for me to make more of them, had diverted my thoughts
from my previous miseries. Perhaps he had just happened along at a particularly favorable time in my career, or perhaps it was the force of his personality that
impressed me, but a faint stirring of intuition told me Mr.
Collins might be of great help in my future career.

I made some more records for him, and bought myself a phonograph so that Mother and I could hear them
at home. I got a great thrill out of seeing my records in
music shops, but although I used to wait around, I never
actually saw anybody buy one. Time spent in this way,
however, was not time spent in worrying about what I
would do when "Flying High" closed.

Mr. Collins took me to supper two or three times in
the next three months and went on talking about records. He opened a whole new world of music for me
with his friendly talks. Then, sometime in November of
1930, he came to see me after the show and was about to
ask me to go out to supper with him when I said, "Not
this time, Mr. Collins. This time you come home to supper with me, for a little of that Southern cooking. My
mother has heard so much about you that she wants to

meet you—and she cooks better than any restaurant chef anywhere."

"Okay, why not? And we can listen to your new record at the same time."

My mother had prepared Southern fried chicken as only she knows how, and we enjoyed a meal full of laughter while we played my records. Then my mother said, as she served dessert, "Have you heard how long 'Flying High's going to run yet, Kathryn?"

Mr. Collins looked at me a little sharply. "What are you going to do then, Kathryn? May I call you Kathryn, by the way?"

"Sure, and can I call you Ted—or would you prefer Edward, or is it Edmund?" I answered, giggling a little.

"It's neither—it's Joseph Martin, but I've never been called by either of them, and if I saw them written down I wouldn't know it was me they referred to."

"How did you get called Ted, then?" asked my mother.

"Well, now, that's funny, that is. My father was a doctor, a physician, you know, and when he was first in practice he used to attend the Roosevelt family—not the Governor's family, but the other Roosevelts. Theodore Roosevelt was born on Twentieth Street, you know. Well, my father admired T.R. very much and when he saw me as a little boy walking very sturdily, just like Teddy Roosevelt, he called me 'little Ted' and I guess it stuck, for I've been called it ever since! But look," he said, pushing his dessert plate away so that he could put his hands on the table and lean toward me, "that's beside the point. What are you going to do when 'Flying High' is through, Kathryn?"

I looked at mother; I had hoped he had forgotten about that. "I'm quitting show business," I said simply. "I'm going back home to Washington."

"What's the matter, don't you like New York?" he asked.

"Oh, yes, I like New York, but——"

"New York's wonderful—it's the most interesting place in the whole world," Ted began. "I've lived here all my life—over on Forty-sixth Street—and I don't want to live anywhere else ever. Where else could you find a group of people living exactly as they would in China, another group living as much as possible as they would in Italy, or in Poland or in Germany, and yet have them all of the same nationality and all crowded together on a small island thirteen miles long? You've got everything here, you can do everything here—I don't care what it is. There's even the real country in Central Park where you can go bird-watching——"

"But you live in the country now, don't you?" asked Mother.

"Yes, but we're going to move back to Manhattan soon. The trip by train's too much for me when I have so many things to watch in New York. Why, you know, I first heard Kathryn because I missed my train out to Rockaway Park and had to kill time until the next one. Perhaps it was a good thing after all."

Mother and I were both under the spell of his attractive voice, so I asked him, "Ted, you've talked to me about records so often—how did you first get interested in them?"

"Ah, heck, Kathryn, I can't remember a time when I didn't know about records. I guess I was the first person who made that terrible joke about only playing the phonograph, but with me it was true!"

"Well, when did you start earning your living by knowing so much? Let's drink our coffee in the arm-chairs, Mother," I said.

As we shifted over and settled ourselves, Ted answered, "When I was at school just after the war I was broke, like all students, so I went into the Columbia Phonograph Company one day. I made as if I wanted a record, but I foxed them all around with what I knew about records so much that eventually I found myself— as I had hoped—talking to the manager. A few days later I got hired as a salesman while I was still at school, and I went on full time when I graduated."

"And you've just gone on from there?" I asked.

"Sure. I was made recording manager when I was twenty-three, which was eight years ago. Someday I think I'll own the company!"

"Well, if ambition'll do it, you will, Mr. Collins," said my mother.

"Do you just go around listening to people like me and getting them to make records?" I asked.

"That's part of it, but I don't always ask them to make

records—only the ones I'm sure are going to be hits. And you, Kathryn, are going to be a hit," he said firmly.

There was silence for a moment. It was broken when Ted got up to leave, saying that he'd have to rush to get the last train out to his home. He noticed the telephone as he went out and wrote down the number.

"I'm lazy," he said. "Why should I always go 'round to the Apollo when I could call you here at home or leave a message with Mrs. Smith? And if I do, I might get invited to have some Southern fried chicken again and that would be grand!"

These meetings and record-making sessions with Ted were the only cheerful interludes in my life, which was increasingly absorbed with worry about what I should do after "Flying High." The situation wasn't helped by the continued unpleasantness of my part and the insistent insults of the comedians, who seemed to get daily more ingenious in their reference to my size. I couldn't help comparing them with Ted, who had never once made any remark about my weight and didn't seem to notice it. He knew I was a singer and treated me accordingly.

In the middle of December a notice was circulated to the members of the cast of "Flying High," saying that in view of the declining attendance, it was probable that the show would close at the end of January, 1931. That evening, groups of people stood in the corridor backstage, talking about the approaching end of the Broadway run, before they went off to their dressing rooms. My nerves were stretched to the breaking point by worry about the decision I knew I would soon have to make, so I wasn't disposed to be very polite when someone hailed me. I recognized the voice of the star. "Hey, Kate, what're you going to do when we're through? Get a job in a circus?"

I couldn't bear it. The tears choked my voice as I lost my temper and shouted at him, "No! I'm going home— I'm getting out of it, to where there aren't any lowdown funny people like you to laugh at the weaknesses of others——" and I fled into my dressing room. It was, of course, the most foolish thing I could have done; I could hear the snickerings outside the door as I dressed.

"What's eating her?" "What's the matter—her boyfriend couldn't get both his arms around her?" "Ah, she can't take it—good thing she's quitting."

The stage that night was for me nothing but a place of torment. They tried everything—and all of it seemed to get laughs. I could hardly sing for tears that would not keep down out of my throat and eyes. When at last it was over and I escaped to my dressing room, I waited until everyone had left the theater before creeping out. How I prayed that I might never have to go back!

When I got home Mother gave me a message from Ted, who had telephoned to ask me to come to his office the next afternoon and hear a couple of records we had made the week before. Even that was no help. All I wanted was to get away to where no one could look at me again, to hide in a corner for the rest of my life. I went to bed after eating only a small part of the supper Mother had made for me.

I did not sleep well, worrying all night long about having to go back to that theater the next day; walking through the stage door would be like dragging legs weighted with chains, and I wondered if I should ever get on the stage or whether I would go mad before I got to the wings. I saw myself sobbing hysterically in my dressing room, with strong arms binding me, while I flailed and twisted, screaming, "No! No! No!" at the top of my voice.

When I got to the Columbia Phonograph Company's offices next day, Ted must have seen at a glance that something was wrong. My face had never looked so gray with misery; I could only just manage a smile for him as he led me to his office and put me in a large armchair opposite his desk.

"Kathryn, listen to this," he said, soothingly, as he sat behind the desk and put my latest record on the phonograph.

"What's the use, Ted, what's the use?" I collapsed all at once and began to cry, sobbing right from my chest, weeping as if it were the last thing in the world I would ever do. Ted stopped the record. He said nothing.

I went on crying. Between sobs I blurted out to him all my troubles: how I had hated being in "Flying High," how I knew I was fat but I didn't see why people thought it so funny, how I had lost my temper with them and couldn't bear the thought of going back that evening.

"But, Ted, oh, Ted," I sobbed, "I want to go on singing, but how can I do it? I can't, I won't be laughed at in a comedy again, but how else can I sing? I don't want to do anything else but sing. Why can't people see me as a singer and not as a stooge? What shall I do? The show's going to close at the end of January and then I'll have to go home and I can't bear that either."

I gave myself up to hopeless weeping. I never again felt so utterly lost until the time, twenty-six years later, when Ted was not there to see or hear me. I was in such a state that for one moment I had the distinct feeling that Ted might slap me to stop my hysteria, as my father had once done. But he just stood in front of me.

"Kathryn, look at me." His voice was never more sincere or more confident. I lifted my head and he smiled at me. "Forget it, Kathryn, it's all over. I'm going to be your manager from now on, and all you'll have to do for the rest of your life is sing."

"What do you mean?"

"Kathryn, do you trust me?"

"Why, yes, Ted, of course."

"Well then, here's what we'll do. When we shake hands, I'll become your manager and take care of everything for you—your bookings, your career, your finances. I'll pick your songs and you'll sing 'em. You won't have anything else ever to worry about but just singing. We'll divide the profits fifty-fifty, which is about the way we'll divide the work."

"Profits?" I said, unable to believe that there was any future for me.

"Yes, Kathryn, you and I are going a long way together. We'll be millionaires before you know what to do with a million dollars. And all you'll have to do is sing—and follow my instructions. Look, here's my hand; when we shake, the deal's on."

I smiled through my tears and put out my hand to meet his. It was the first time I had shaken hands with him; his grip was firm and it filled me with confidence.

"All right, Ted. It's a deal," I said.

Four

THAT handshake was the only contract Ted and I have ever made. We signed no papers, we saw no lawyers, and we have never done these things since. And from that moment I felt secure, knowing that every decision Ted made about my career would be the right one.

He even had a solution for my immediate dilemma. We listened to the records I had made while I recovered my composure completely. Then, leaning forward over his desk, Ted said, "Those are good records, Kate, but we won't make our fortune with them yet because not enough people buy them."

"Well, what am I going to do then? 'Flying High' closes at the end of January," I began, but I suddenly re-

membered how I had suffered the previous evening. The
new vistas opened up by Ted's becoming my manager
had made me forget it temporarily. "Oh, Ted, I don't
know how I'm going to go back to that show. Couldn't
I just not go ever again and let an understudy take the
part?"

He smiled and shook his head. "Kathryn, a manager
has disciplinary duties as well as promotional ones, and
now I'm your manager, I'm afraid I'm not going to let
you get away with it so easily. Besides, it wouldn't look
good if people could say in the future that Kate Smith
couldn't take it, would it? No, you'll have to stay with
'Flying High' until the end of the run——"

"But I can't bear it——" I began.

"Now wait a minute, Kathryn. I'm not throwing you
to the wolves. I'm going to go along there this evening
before the show and talk to a few people as your manager, and I'll bet there won't be a scene again after I do."

"I don't see how that will do much good," I said
despondently.

"Wait and see, Kathryn, wait and see. Now then,
when 'Flying High' ends, I think you should go home
to Washington for a long vacation."

"What about my apartment in New York?" I asked,
always practical where money was concerned.

"Keep that on—you can afford it, can't you? I
haven't yet decided what we're going to do when you
come back to New York, but I have several things in

mind. You can bet you're going to need that apartment," he said.

When I went to the Apollo Theatre that evening, there was a different atmosphere altogether. There was no greater cordiality than before, and no one apologized to me (which would have been in its way very painful), but there were no further attempts to bait me. Even the ad-libs in the show were kept to a minimum and were not of the worst variety. This change was caused by two things: Ted's visit, which certainly had the effect he intended, and my own confidence that the future was assured. As soon as Ted became my manager, my troubles seemed halved; the last few weeks of "Flying High" went quickly and I felt sure of myself once more.

At last I was able to go home to Washington for a vacation, leaving the future entirely in Ted's hands. During the next six weeks I came up to New York two or three times to make records for the Columbia Phonograph Company, but Ted never mentioned any future plans on these occasions. I could tell, however, that something was in the air, but I asked no questions.

My grandparents were very happy to see me in Washington, of course, but still could not understand my desire to go on singing. When I told them of my arrangement with Ted, they were astounded that I should trust a man whom I had not known even a year. I believe, from later chance conversations, that my grandfather began looking around among his acquaintances for a suitable employer for me, although I do not know what he imagined I could do except sing. Mother, of course, had met Ted and understood my great faith in his judgment; she also had a soothing confidence in my ambitions that helped a great deal.

About the middle of March, 1931, when I was feeling fully rested and much refreshed from my vacation, Ted called me on the telephone. He asked me to pack everything and come back to New York prepared to stay some time.

"How are you feeling, Kathryn?" he asked.

"Oh, I feel great, really great, Ted. What is it we're going to do?"

"Well, I'm glad you're in good shape, because you're going to be quite busy. You're going to sing at the Capitol Theater five times a day for a good many weeks," he said with a chuckle in his voice.

"But isn't the Capitol a movie theater?" I asked.

"Sure, but they're going to have a season of showing a movie followed by a stage show—and you're going to be the featured singer. Come on, Kathryn, stop talking and get up here—we'll arrange everything then."

I was beaming as I put the phone down and ran to tell Mother. We spent the rest of the day packing excitedly, while I sang snatches of the songs I wanted to do. Mother came with me on this trip to New York, leaving my sister alone for a few days. I couldn't help reminding her that there was a curious parallel to this departure for New York and the one when I was seventeen and was

84

to appear in "Honeymoon Lane." On both occasions I was setting out to do something quite new and wasn't sure of the outcome.

"But there is something different, Kathryn," said Mother gently. "This time you have a manager."

In my apartment in New York we had a conference, at which Ted told me the arrangements he had made with the management of the Capitol.

"They want you to sing the popular favorites, of course," he said, "but I've persuaded them to let me choose which ones for you. And then you can do some of the old sweet songs—something like 'Silver Threads Among the Gold.'"

"I'm so glad you got those," I answered. "I think I like singing them even better than the new songs. But, Ted, how should I sing them?"

"Kathryn, that's up to you. I only said I'd pick them. Is there any way to sing a song but exactly as the composer wrote it? I've heard you when you're recording and I know that you have a perfect ear for tune and rhythm, so I'll leave the singing to you. Just enjoy yourself."

"What should I do about clothes?" I asked.

"Oh, get a few evening gowns made. What do you usually do?"

"Well, I have a dressmaker, but I'd feel much better if you took a look at them," I answered.

"Okay, I'll come down to a fitting one day. But you'd better hustle, for you start next Monday and it's Tuesday now. You'll have to go to the Capitol for an orchestra rehearsal Friday afternoon and possibly Sunday as well. Perhaps you'd better call that dressmaker now and warn her."

The next day I spent nearly all my time at the dressmaker's, choosing materials and styles. Then on Thursday I went to Ted's office and chose exactly which songs I should sing at the Capitol. Friday morning was spent at the hairdresser's, trying the latest style. It was a great joy to be able to go on the stage looking my best instead of having to conform to the ideas of a wardrobe mistress and designer.

Ted noticed my new hairdo at the rehearsal at once and complimented me on it.

"That's great, Kathryn, makes you look younger even than you are. Get that fellow to do it for you every day, and maybe switch things a little after a week or two, you know?"

Next morning I asked him to drop in at the dressmaker's while I tried on a couple of the gowns I had ordered. He looked critically at one which had short sleeves.

"No, Kathryn, don't wear short sleeves. Yes, I know it's the fashion, but it doesn't flatter you. The sleeves can be made longer, can't they? And I think that neck's a bit severe, cut across like that. Let's have it as open as possible—you've got lovely skin, show it off."

He never failed to encourage me with a little flattery. Looking at one dress he said, "You look great in that,

Kathryn. The black lace looks so rich and it flows behind you when you walk. That'd be a good style to copy in other colors."

When I sang for the first time at the Capitol on Monday, Ted was standing in the wings. I went out there confident in my new dress and hairdo and sang just as if I were singing only for him at a recording session. As I had predicted, I thoroughly enjoyed it. Even the hard work of singing at five shows a day didn't detract from the pleasure. After a week or two, we varied the songs by arrangement with the management, but the essence of them remained the same—a medley of new and old songs sung straight, exactly as the composer had intended. The audiences seemed to enjoy them as much as I did.

I had been singing at the Capitol for about six weeks, with the audience increasing every day, when Ted came 'round to my dressing room after the show one afternoon. I had showered and dressed and was enjoying the short rest I usually took before going out for a few minutes between shows.

"You've got a surprise, Ted," I said, looking at the sparkle in his eyes.

"Okay, if I look like a man who's just brought off a lifelong ambition, it's because I have. You're going to be on radio, Kathryn," he announced.

"Me? When? But I can't, the thing you sing into will freeze me and the thought of all those people listening—"

"The thought of all those people will just make you sing better. I've arranged with Columbia for you to have a fifteen-minute program every evening at seven o'clock, five days a week. Congratulate me! It was tough persuading those guys you're going to be good."

"Oh, I do, Ted! How did you do it?"

"I made them listen to your records, I brought them around to hear you here when you didn't know, I showed them the receipts in the manager's office. And I talked to them——"

A thought had struck me and I interrupted him: "Ted! You said seven o'clock in the evening, didn't you? But that's Amos 'n' Andy time on NBC! Ted, that's ridiculous! No one will even know I'm on the air."

He got up from his chair and walked behind it. "Kathryn, inside a year the public won't know Amos 'n' Andy are on the air, that's what."

"Now, look, that's plain silly. I'm completely unknown and they're part of radio. Couldn't you have picked a better time than that for me to begin, one when there wasn't so much competition?" I was really worried about starting in opposite such a popular show.

He lifted his hand and slapped it down on the back of the chair. "Kathryn, you've got to learn that when Collins says a thing will happen, it will happen. I deliberately chose that time because I think if there's a challenge to be met, the time to meet it is right away. If we can buck Amos 'n' Andy, we can buck anything, and I'd rather know this now than later."

I felt a bit meek, but reassured. "All right, Ted, now when is the great day?"

"Next week, May first," he said, sitting back in his chair again.

"My, what a fine birthday present that'll be for me— a first class case of nerves!"

"How old will you be, Kathryn?"

"Twenty-one. And Mother won't be here either, she's going back home tomorrow for a week or two."

"All the better, she can hear you at home and get a much bigger thrill that way. Now look, come down to my office at Columbia tomorrow and we'll go over some songs for the program. And don't think about it too much. In fact, I've known for a few days now, but I haven't told you because I didn't want you to worry too long."

In Ted's office next day we had sheets of music spread all over the desk. We had to pick five songs, which we thought would just fill fifteen minutes, and then we would give them to the accompanist to play through. It was to be a very simple program—just my voice and a five-piece band.

We soon decided on four songs, which I had often sung before and liked very much: "By the River St. Marie," "I Surrender Dear," "Please Don't Talk About Me When I'm Gone," and "Dream a Little Dream Of Me."

"Well, we need one more and it ought to be a sort of theme song—you know, a bit at the beginning and a bit at the end," said Ted, tapping a pencil on the desk. "I don't like any of these for it. It ought to be something new, something we can identify with you, Kathryn."

I raked over the music sheets and brought up one we'd had in the office for some time.

"Look at this one, Ted, 'When the Moon Comes Over the Mountain,'" and I hummed a few bars as he looked at the sheet.

"I like that, Kathryn. Sing it for me properly."

I sang it through and laughed as I came to the end.

"You know, I helped to write that song," I told Ted. "Then nobody seemed to like it and I've just carried it around with me, hoping to use it one day. Do you really like it?"

"Sure, I do. It's got all we need—a suggestion of something new, a good sweeping melody, and your own connection with it. Let's have it."

So we had our program filled with songs, but I was worried about what I thought of as the frame for it.

"You know, Ted, I don't like these elaborate introductions people do on the radio. They spoil my pleasure and I guess they spoil things for a lot of other people. But on the other hand, I can't just start singing—there has to be some explanation of who I am."

"I thought the same thing, Kathryn. We want to make this very simple so that it will strike a new note in radio. That's the way to get noticed over Amos 'n' Andy. I think you should just come right on and say 'Hello everybody. This is Kate Smith.'"

We started to clear up the mess of sheet music on the desk. I stopped suddenly and said, "Oh, and by the way, Ted, I completely forgot to ask you what the contract pays us."

He laughed. "You sure trust me, Kathryn, but I wouldn't have got rich on this one even if I'd run away with the lot. We're getting ten dollars a program from CBS, because we have no sponsor as yet. But when we get one, I expect we'll make real money."

"If we get one——" I said pensively.

"*When* we get one, Kathryn. Remember, if Collins says we will——"

"I know—we will! I'll believe you," I said, as we both laughed.

Ted picked me up in a taxi after my fourth show at the Capitol on the day of the program. I had one more show to do that evening after my broadcast, and then I had to do a special midnight matinee for a benefit, so my birthday wasn't exactly spent restfully. In the taxi on the way to the studio Ted scribbled the words I was to say at the beginning and the end of the program on a piece of paper, just so nerves would not dry me up completely. And we ran over the order of my songs once more.

The studio seemed deadly quiet to me and I felt the palms of my hands get sticky as nerves overtook me once more. An engineer showed me where to stand in front of the microphone, not very close to it, but near enough to get all my voice. I stood there watching the studio clock tell off the remaining seconds until I was on the air, twisting a scarf between my fingers to keep myself calm. Ted stood by me, holding the piece of paper with my words on it and reassuring me, "I'm glad the mike frightens you, Kathryn, because that means you're going to be good. Once you've had mike fright and gotten over it, it never troubles you again."

At last the hands of the clock moved around to seven exactly and the red light flashed on to tell me I was on the air. From somewhere miles away, it seemed, I heard the music begin and then my own voice—although it didn't seem as if it belonged to me. I went right through the routine exactly as we had planned it, my eyes fixed on that red light, which I was certain would never go off. It would remain there for ever and I would have to go on singing, singing, holding notes, trying to fill time . . .

It did go off—and exactly at the second I finished saying "Thanks for listening." I wiped the perspiration from my face and turned to Ted, limp with relief.

He held up both his hands clasped like a victorious boxer.

"Swell," he said. Then I noticed that the rest of the people in the studio were smiling too.

Within the next ten minutes, people began telephoning. The switchboard operator told Ted later that the board lit up "like the sky on an old-fashioned Fourth of July." People all around New York were calling to say how much they enjoyed the simplicity of the program and the songs—and asking for more. One of the calls was from Mother in Washington. They put it through in an office where Ted and I were recovering before I went back to the Capitol.

"Congratulations, Kathryn," came my mother's voice over the wire. "You gave yourself a lovely birthday present. It sounded wonderful here—just as if you were singing for us alone."

"Thanks, Mother, I guess I was singing for you. It's marvelous to think I'm being heard in people's homes, part of the family."

"Kathryn, your Granny was here listening too and she wants to talk to you."

A voice full of tears and emotion said, "Oh, Kathryn, it was lovely hearing you all those miles away. I was really proud. And you sang such sweet songs. I think maybe you were right to stick to it after all."

My own throat thickened as I said, "I'm so glad you enjoyed it, Granny. Maybe radio was the answer, but we'll have to wait and see."

We only had to wait until the next morning to see the first of our fan mail and to find out how much my simple singing had been really appreciated. I went to Ted's office, and there the two of us opened every letter we received—something which hasn't been possible since because of the heavy volume of mail. But this was very special, for these letters meant that people had taken the trouble to write to encourage a girl of twenty-one who was completely unknown to them. I sat there smiling broadly with a pile of paper and envelopes in my lap.

"Ted, isn't it wonderful? Why did they do it? You know, I don't think if I were someone in a small country town in upper New York State I'd take the trouble to write to a radio singer whom I'd never met, would you? But it's marvelous that these people did!"

He looked wisely at me from behind the desk and answered, "Kathryn, we'd be in trouble now if they hadn't. You can see why they write, I think, if you remember what your mother said last night over the phone—it was just as if you were singing in the living room for her alone. All these people heard your voice right there in the family circle and they thought of you as a friend. That's the feeling we've got to preserve, and they'll never want to hear the last of you."

We put the letters away—some of them very carefully, for I wanted to keep them—and went on to choose four songs for that evening's broadcast. We only needed four, for "When the Moon Comes Over the Mountain" was going to stay in its place as my theme song.

Within thirty days of beginning the fifteen-minute program, we had a sponsor, La Palina Cigars, paying me $1500 a week. At about the same time, my engagement at the Capitol Theater came to an end and I was able to devote my whole day to looking through songs to find suitable ones for the broadcast. Then organizations and individuals—men, women, children, folks in hospitals—began to send in requests for me to sing songs for them, and the programming became easier and easier. To top it all off, within six months the competition I had dreaded so much, "Amos 'n' Andy," was moved to a different time to avoid competing with me.

My trust in Ted's judgment was completely justified. And he proved his faith in me by giving up his job with the Columbia Phonograph Company and becoming my manager on a full-time basis. Together we formed a corporation we called Kated from our two names, and hired people to work for it. After a month or two of the daily program, it became obvious that the two of us with only an occasional hour or two at the typewriter could not cope with the work involved, so we hired secretaries to deal with the mail, a full-time accompanist, and an arranger, and we took an office. Within a few years, Kated was employing some sixty or seventy people, including a band.

The newspapers were continually asking me for interviews, but rather than give them individually and keep repeating the answers to the same questions, Ted organized a press conference in our new office. Representatives of all the New York newspapers came, and I found myself answering exceedingly personal questions. Ted sat at my side, occasionally whispering to me; he never contradicts me in public.

When the reporters, including quite a number of

women in the soft suits and floopy hats of that year, were all settled and had taken out their pads and pencils, the barrage started.

"Where were you born, Miss Smith?" asked one young man.

"In Greenville, Virginia," I answered.

"When did you first sing in public?" asked another.

"Gee, I can't remember. I was a member of the local church choir at a very early age, and I guess I just went on from there."

"What's your religion, then?" he went on.

"Oh, I'm a Catholic," I answered. "When I got a little older, I was a member of the St. Pat's Players in Washington, D.C."

"But you didn't sing in a Catholic church choir, surely?" This young man was obviously keen to get to the bottom of things.

"No, but my family is half Catholic and half Protestant, and we went to the Protestant church as well as the Catholic one," I answered, a little unwillingly. I found it difficult to talk of such personal things. If only they'd stick to musical questions, I thought.

"How many meals a day do you eat, Miss Smith?" asked one of the women, who probably ran a food column.

"The usual three," I answered, wondering if I was supposed to eat twice as much as anyone else. "I eat a light breakfast, maybe an apple for lunch, and then I eat a big meal very late in the evening after all my singing is through for the day. You can't sing on a full stomach."

"You don't diet then?" she went on.

"No, I don't see any need to. I just take as much exercise as I can, walking to the studio, swimming whenever possible—singing's an exercise in itself, you know."

"What advice would you give to a beginner in radio, Miss Smith?" came one of the last questions.

"I guess I'm only a beginner myself yet," I answered laughing, "but the best advice for anyone would be to get a manager like Ted Collins!"

They all shuffled out, chatting to one another, picking up hats and notebooks. As the door closed behind the last reporter, Ted groaned and slapped his forehead. "Why didn't you tell them Washington, D.C., instead of Greenville, Kathryn? Now we'll have you claimed by Greenville as a native daughter and you don't know a soul there! I bet you don't even know what the main street looks like."

"Oh, I never thought of that."

"I guess there's some dividend in it—you'll get called the songbird of the South, or something like that. But it'll make for confusion."

He was, of course, right about the confusion over my birthplace. I did get called the Songbird of the South and it took some years to live it down. Greenville did try to claim me, and I felt very uncomfortable that I had no ties there. And in some reference books my birthplace is listed as Greenville, some as Washington. Since then I have mostly left interviews and stories for newspapers to Ted, who sees more clearly what will happen when information is given to a reporter.

The newness and excitement of becoming a radio personality stayed with me throughout the rest of that year. There was always a letter which thrilled me because it asked me to do a favorite song; then there was a song Ted had heard somewhere and thought would be good for me; then there would be a frantic search for a different song when we tired of the usual ones. I was always singing—rehearsing new songs, reviving old ones. And there was always Ted, encouraging, criticizing, suggesting new ideas.

One Saturday we spent the whole morning in our office going over possible songs for the program. Time passed as swiftly as it always did when we were completely absorbed in our work. Then I went off to the hairdresser for my weekly session. Since I had gone on radio, there was no longer any need to have my hair done every day as there had been when I appeared on the stage. I came home to my apartment late in the afternoon and put on the radio, for it seemed a little lonely; my mother had gone home to Washington for that weekend because my sister was suffering from a cold and needed care. I wandered into the kitchen and decided to keep myself cheerful by making something really elaborate for dinner. I love cooking and believe in being very exact about measurements and timing, so that preparing a meal is a very absorbing business for me, guaranteed to take my mind off being alone.

Next morning, I remained in bed a little later than usual. When the telephone rang, I thought it was my mother from Washington, and for a moment I wondered if Helene, my sister, was worse. I lifted the receiver beside my bed and heard a voice I did not immediately recognize.

"Hello, Kathryn. This is Jeannette Collins. Look, Ted and I completely forgot yesterday that you were alone this weekend with your mother away. Would you like to come over here for Sunday lunch?"

"Why, sure, Jeannette, that's great."

"Fine. Come over after you've been to church—doesn't matter if lunch isn't ready then—just come on over."

As soon as I began to earn what might be called fairly large sums, I bought a car and began to explore the country around New York. In the summers I went further afield, and discovered Lake Placid in upper New York State. There I fell completely in love with the mountains reflected in the lake, the fir trees standing around the edge of the water, the clearness of the blue sky. It seemed an ideal place to which to retreat for the summer from the stifling atmosphere of New York. When I could afford it, I bought an island in the middle of the lake and built a camp on it. Now there are three houses on that island—my own, one belonging to the

Collins family, and another belonging to a doctor. I began to spend all summer up there, going up about the beginning of June and returning a couple of weeks after Labor Day. The island is ideally situated because it ensures my privacy without my having to protect myself with fences.

Later during the thirties I discovered more of the country on our tours. At the end of 1932 Ted took me to Hollywood to make a film, which was called "Hello Everybody!" I didn't much like the movie capital, as I'm not fond of parties and staying up late, but I did appreciate the opportunity to see the West Coast. During the next year the whole Kated Corporation took off for an extensive road tour calling itself the "Swanee Revue." I loved appearing on the stage again after two years as an unseen voice; it seemed impossible that I had once been miserable at the thought of stepping onto a stage for fear of being laughed at.

My life went on getting bigger and bigger during the rest of the decade. Within two years of my first program, we were offered an hour show on Thursday evenings and my earnings went up to $5000 a week. This program took a great deal of work, for there was a dramatic spot in which stars of the stage and the movies acted a short play; a comedy spot, which among other things gave Abbott and Costello their first break in radio; several arrangements for my songs, and usually an interview. We also began raising money for various good causes, and we never stopped being surprised at how much money listeners were willing to part with in those hard times to help others.

Ted was grooming me during these years for a new part, although I didn't realize it until the spring of 1938. We were together in his office, which then overlooked Columbus Circle at 1819 Broadway. We had been laughing and chatting, when he suddenly walked to the door and closed it, so that the rest of the staff would not hear our conversation. He came back to the desk and sat on it, his legs swinging.

"Kathryn, we're going to start something new next week—something we've never done before."

"All right, what is it? An interview with a performing seal? What's the matter, Ted? You always have an itch for something new. Aren't things fine as they are?"

"Sure, they are, but you know very well you've got to keep on changing, keeping one jump ahead of the public so they don't get tired before you do. This time, Kathryn, you're going to do a commentary program. No singing, just straight talking."

I sat down and stared at him. "Ted, this is really tough. The public knows me as a singer."

"It isn't so tough, Kathryn. Sure they know you as a singer, but they also know you as an interviewer and as a sponsor for good causes."

"But you can't make a program out of that."

"I don't intend to. Look, we read the newspapers every morning, don't we? And when we do, I often hear you say about such-and-such a thing, 'Boy, this makes my blood boil—it's unjust.' That's the sort of thing the program's going to be made of—your comments on the news, in those ordinary conversational terms."

"Fine, Simon Legree—on we go. When do I start?"

"April fourth. It'll only be three times a week at first, and then I expect we'll have to go to five days a week."

"And if Collins expects a thing to happen—it will!"

Not surprisingly, it did. The commentator program, as we came to call it, eventually became a regular daily feature of American life from noon until 12:15 every day. I enjoyed doing it very much, but it was tremendously hard work for everyone in the office. We installed two special United Press teletype machines in the office, on one of which we got the ordinary news, and on the other, human interest stories which soon became my specialty. Ted would be in the office first thing in the morning, looking at the news on these machines; then he would read through the newspapers for additional suitable items. When he had decided on the content of the program, he would either write what I was to say himself, or give it to one of Kated's writers to do, and later check it himself. The mail might also bring a good idea for a comment, and one person in the office had the special responsibility of looking for interesting letters. The whole program would be rounded up about mid-morning, and then Ted would take a taxi to my apartment, where we would go over the script and I would add what I had found interesting in the papers that morning.

At noon we went on the air from my apartment, there being no need to use a studio for a one-woman broadcast. At first I read the news and the commercials, but later I turned the news reading over to Ted, who proceeded to make a name for himself as a newscaster over the years. In the afternoons we would collect material for future commentator broadcasts and arrange our hour-long show, which was now on Friday evenings. That had to be performed twice, once at eight o'clock in the evening and again at midnight so that it could be heard out on the West Coast. The pace was so killing that I know Ted sometimes only got four hours' sleep a night. At first we had the summer months in which to rest, but at the beginning of the 1940's we began broadcasting the commentator program from Lake Placid as well, so there was no break at all during the year. That Ted's heart attack did not come until 1956 now seems a miracle to me.

For myself, I never noticed the pace at which we worked because I was enjoying myself so much. Whenever there was any praise or appreciation, I got it, and praise has a way of greatly relieving fatigue and routine. The culmination of this period, the moment which made all the effort seem more than worth it, came one June evening in 1939. Amid the glitter and sparkle of the East Room of the White House, I stood before two people whose lives were surrounded by such glamour that I had never before believed them to be real. But they were: Queen Elizabeth of England had a round smiling face with a very happy expression, and King George VI was handsome with serious blue eyes. As I curtseyed deeply, the warm voice of President Roosevelt at my side said:

"Your Majesties, this is Kate Smith—this is America."

Five

ON MONDAY, December 9, 1940, I did not do my usual noontime commentator program. Ted did it for me. I was at home in Washington acting as maid of honor for my sister, Helene, at her wedding. I have always believed, in spite of my devotion to my work, that family ties take precedence over everything else. My experience with George White at the time of my father's death strengthened this conviction. Whenever there was a great event in the Smith family, I always left the program to Ted and went to Washington to participate in it.

The wedding took place in the evening in our old Washington family home. There wasn't much room for all the relatives and friends who crowded into the living room and dining room, but the crush only added to the fun of the festivity. We all decided it was advisable to have the wedding at home rather than in a church because I knew my appearance as maid of honor would probably draw a great deal of attention; it was my sister's day, and I felt it would be unfair for her to be neglected by crowds who came to stare at her sister.

The wedding was really one great Smith party, with lots of singing to the accompaniment of the piano, comic speech-making, eating, and general merriment. Helene wore a short-skirted party dress in the new fashion of 1940 and had flowers in her hair. Her groom looked just uncomfortable enough in his tuxedo. Granny Hanby wore a silk dress that added to her natural dignity; she had tiny pearls in her ears, her only concession to adorning her face for the occasion, for she would not alter her hair style or powder her cheeks. Grandpa wore the stiff black suit that we knew emerged only from his closet for weddings and funerals. His gold watch-chain gleamed across his vest as he stood proudly beside Helene and her new husband to toast their health.

In the midst of the bustle and laughter, I watched Helene blush as family friends claimed a kiss from the bride; then she and her husband cut the cake and we all applauded as the first slice was served. Quite suddenly I realized as I looked at Helene's happy face that I was terribly happy for her, yet not at all unhappy for myself. Perhaps it was an extraordinary thing to be faced with, as an unmarried woman of thirty-one, but it became more and more true as the fun of the wedding festivities went on—I felt no hurt about not being married myself. I remember realizing that "God fulfills Himself in many ways," and life offers compensations to each of us.

I thought back to a similar wedding scene more than ten years before, when my childhood friend Barbara was married in Washington. Then we had been invited to the wedding in a local church and I had snatched a weekend from the "Hit the Deck" tour between two cities to attend it. Barbara was a young bride and had the full glory of a long white gown and trailing lace veil. I wondered and worried about myself then. Would I ever marry? I could so clearly imagine myself—a much thinner, idealized self—standing at the altar and whispering "I do" with a modest glance at my husband, who of course would be tall, handsome and rich. At the reception I had stolen away to another room to wipe away my tears; it seemed so utterly hopeless that I would ever be as happy as Barbara was that day.

Now, in our living room, old friends came up to me and said, "When do we come to your wedding, Kathryn?" and I was able to reply with a genuine laugh, "What do you want another for—isn't one enough in a family?" The truth of the situation, that I would most probably never have a wedding, had no power to hurt me, and my laugh covered no bitterness.

When my sister left to take up her new life, my mother and I sat down to rest in the deserted living room. We were surrounded by the debris of the party, but since I had to leave on a very early morning train in time to get back to New York for the Tuesday broadcast at noon, Mother decided to forget the mess until I was gone. She sighed as she settled in her chair.

"Well, that's one daughter off my hands. At least there's a chance I'll see my grandchildren!"

"Seems like an ideal situation to me," I answered cheerfully, "one daughter happily married and the other a happy spinster. Just enough grandchildren and not too many."

She turned to me. "Are you really a happy spinster, Kathryn? Is there such a thing?"

"Mom, you have a married woman's prejudice that it isn't possible to be happy without a man in the house. But it most certainly is possible and many women besides me are the living proof. You know, it's a funny thing, but right in the middle of the party I realized that I didn't envy Helene."

"But you must have thought about it before and realized that . . . that . . ."

"That I'd probably never get married? I guess I've just been too busy ever since we started in radio to give it a thought. But a lot of things have become clearer since then—things I guess I've known subconsciously for a long time, but never faced consciously before."

I began telling her the reasons why I felt I was perfectly happy though not married, and before we realized it, hours had slipped away. I got back to New York the next day feeling tired after very little sleep, but with that curiously clean sensation of having marked a stage in my development. Throughout the next few weeks I noticed more and more instances of the way in which I had, without knowing it, successfully adapted to the prospect of not marrying. I went on telling them to Mother, who, since she no longer had my sister to look after, came to live with me permanently in New York.

The night of the wedding I pointed out to her that in the ten years in which my professional career had made phenomenal gains, my aims and ideals had changed. During the period when I was on the musical comedy stage before I was twenty-one—the time of Barbara's wedding—I had the dreams of all young girls: marriage, a home, and family. My dreams had their own variation, of course: my husband, when he came along, would be a singing star—perhaps an operatic tenor or baritone—and our courtship would be spent singing duets. Our wedding would be hailed by the press and our audiences as an ideal union of talents, but after the ceremony, I would probably drop from the public scene and devote myself to furthering my husband's career. I believe firmly in the wife's remaining a support to her husband rather than becoming his public rival; had I married, I would almost certainly have given up my career.

In my dream life, I would entertain brilliantly for my husband, of course, but our greatest pleasure would be in the intimate supper I would prepare for him at the end of a day; I would have spent many hours thinking of a special menu and then preparing it with all the skill and precision I could muster.

When our children came along, they would, naturally, be musical genuises, most probably child prodigies. But in spite of offers from the managements of concert halls, we would see to it that our children had thoroughly normal lives before being exposed to the rigors of concert performance. Consequently they would be mature individuals as well as brilliant musicians. The son who would be a composer would have a depth to his compositions coming from a harmony with life; the daughter who was to become a magnificent soprano would be quite content in her turn to give up her career and further her husband's when the right (and naturally, brilliant) son-in-law came our way.

In the end, for one's dreams are often complete right down to the last detail, Mother Kathryn would become a smiling and serene grandmother, enjoying her declining years surrounded by an ever-increasing family, at the side of a gray-haired but still distinguished husband. Just before our end came—we would probably die within a day or two of one another—we would see our first great-grandchild, and know that our musical gifts would be carried on for many years to come.

The dream had its youthful exaggerations, of course, but it was no more than the average young girl sees as her future. The essentials—a husband to whom to minister in every way, numbers of children and grandchildren to love, laugh at and scold—were there. But as the years went on the dream faded. It did not die an abrupt death, it did not haunt me and then suddenly disappear; it just stopped being dreamed very often and finally was not dreamed at all. In its place came other dreams and fantasies in which the principal figure was myself, not a husband, and the only others were friends and audiences. I saw myself now alone on a stage, a great success, bringing happiness to others with my voice; alone in my apartment enjoying my possessions, rich in friends, talent and fame.

This dream, too, had its day and faded, for with the coming of success in radio, it ceased to be necessary to me. Time for dreaming was at a premium in any case. Reality had broken through all dreams and it was such a good reality that no dream was needed as an escape from it. Success had a lot to do with it, but so had maturity. With the coming of maturity, a woman, even a single woman, learns to stop dreaming and turn her inward eye directly on the present, the here and now. If she is wise enough to have plenty to do, reality is better than any dream.

I said this to my mother. "You know, Mom, it's as if my mental processes had changed gear like a car going up a hill. I don't wonder now what's going to happen to me, whether I'm going to be rich or poor, married or unmarried. I think about what I'm doing today and perhaps tomorrow—what I'll say about the war in Europe this noon, or about President Roosevelt's chat on another day."

"But what about women who haven't got a very happy present?" asked Mother. "You know, women who haven't got enough to do. They'll still go on dreaming."

"Each person must learn to dream with her head, not only with her heart. We all must make for ourselves a way of life. There is only a greater challenge when that way of life doesn't fall into the usual categories. You either take the challenge or you don't. If any woman isn't happy, I believe it's within her power to do something about it. I don't say it's always easy but women are doing it every day. There are so many facets to a full life."

I was grateful that I had been blessed with enough to do. In my house at Lake Placid there is a small plaque on my bedroom wall and it reads:

"Thank God every morning when you get up that you have something to do that day which must be done, whether you like it or not. Being forced to work and forced to do your best will breed in you a hundred virtues the idle will never know."

And I do not think it is by any means impossible for any woman, no matter what her age and station in life, to find enough to do every day and feel that what she does is essential to someone besides herself.

Single women these days too often feel left out of a

family, but it's as much their fault as the family's. If they were only sure that they had something to offer and could get rid of the idea that they are super-fluous, they would be much more interesting as people. A happy aunt who directs a child's interest to museums, zoos, or books can be an incalculable influence for good on a child and give him a different experience with adults from that which he receives from his parents.

I think the first thing single women of any age need in order to feel fully alive and happy is to rid themselves of the idea that by not being married they have failed. Our society is far too insistent upon marriage as a mark of success; this attitude does great harm, for it not only necessitates a defensive attitude in the un-married, but also tends to rush young people into mar-riage before they are fully prepared for it.

There are two important things to remember about single women: one is that because of the surplus of women, it is actually impossible for a large number of women to find husbands; the second is that frequently a woman who feels a vocation toward a career deliber-ately chooses not to be married in order to give her full time and energy to her work. In view of these two facts, feelings of failure among unmarried women are both unnecessary and harmful.

Right now, there are about two million more women than men in the United States. Those two million girls were apparently destined never to have the protection and guidance of a husband; they'll have to stand on their own two feet throughout a life which will last longer than women's lives have ever lasted—some of them into the twenty-first century. In more primitive societies in the Middle East where women outnumbered men even more, polygamy did provide almost every woman with at least a fraction of a husband, but our society has never sanctioned harems and even the Moslems are now turning away from this old custom.

What good will it do for these two million women to regard themselves as failures because they didn't get married? Far better to face the facts and be proud that they can support themselves and live rich lives. The sympathy of friends is misplaced; whispers of, "She never did catch a man, poor dear, but she's very sensible about it" only increase the problem. There is a need for a different attitude on the part of society toward the unmarried woman; she should not be regarded as a kind of freak, but as a perfectly normal person with the same hopes, wishes, and ambitions as anyone else. She has merely fulfilled them differently.

I am very disturbed by the modern pressures of advertising and magazine writing which insist on life as one long jolly round of parties and "fun." Advertisements for soft drinks and cigarettes emphasize gatherings of rosy-cheeked young people perpetually dancing to phonograph records; those for washing-machines show how dyeing can be done in your party dress; huge automobiles are always swooping off on long superhighways toward mythical paradises; the words "happy," "young," "party," "fun," pop out at you from full-page advertisements or from block-long billboards. And on television, when a man wants you to buy anything from an oven cleaner to aluminum foil, he smiles, smiles, smiles, so that I begin to count his teeth after a while. The presentation of news on radio and in the newspapers is brightened up to a point where it is often difficult to follow what actually happened. The result of our continually being told that life is just a bowl of cherries and that we must be happy all the time is that, whether we like it or not, we gradually begin to believe it. And if we expect to be happy all the time, we are hurt and angry when we're not. The unmarried woman is doubly a victim of this pressure. She is told she must be happy all the time, but happiness is equated with marriage and a family.

I am not advocating a more solemn attitude to life, just a more realistic one. It's becoming more and more difficult to ignore exhortations to dance your life away, since they are forced on you by radio, television, newspapers, magazines, the wrappings on the goods you buy, and the mail which comes through your door; however, it is well to remember that the only people who are happy twenty-four hours a day live in a fantasy world. Ordinary everyday life has its quota of happiness, of frustration, of surprise, of dull routine, even of unavoidable misery; the well-adjusted adult faces the facts of his life and tries to take everything as it comes. Such an adult also recognizes that a party, or an occasion on which "happiness" is supposed to flourish, is much more enjoyable when it comes as a contrast to hard work instead of as a steady diet.

Many a frightened, immature single woman actually fears unhappiness long before it comes, because she has been conditioned to expect to be happy. She fears being alone, thinking of loneliness as the curse of being single; she forgets that a married woman can be just as alone as she is. She envies her married friends, thinking that happiness comes automatically with a husband; she doesn't realize that a good marriage requires as great an adjustment as does any other way of life. She must accept and learn to live with her occasional loneliness, unhappiness and envy as a normal part of her life. The single woman who is emotionally well-balanced and therefore can give her best to her job and to the people around her is one who looks straight at reality and says, "I am unmarried, but not ashamed, and I am going to live my life to the full, like any other adult."

While I'm shaping up the world as I'd like it, I'd also like to see an effort made in education toward ensuring that the right women remain unmarried; I mean those best qualified to stand on their own feet. Too much of the stigma attached to the single state has been caused by the obvious unfitness of some women to live the single life. Certain types of women are better suited for life on their own than others; shy, yielding girls who are hesitant in making up their minds and scared of new things would clearly be happier married than they would be working in offices, whereas a girl with marked talent and ambition could probably be just as happy following her star. I say only "probably" because, under the present pressures of society, she would feel herself bound to try to get a husband as well. But if a teacher or school psychologist had told her during her formative years that she would be one of the women strong enough to stand on her own, she might be conditioned to a single life early enough to prevent frustration. The energy usually directed to finding a husband could be used to improve her abilities. It is a matter of changing the expectation that a girl will be married into the possibility that she will not. If this is done early enough, she will suffer no embarrassment at being single even when many of her friends get engaged and married, and her self-confidence will be built up so that envy of her married companions is reduced to a minimum.

Such a woman, occupied by a career which absorbs her, enjoying many friends, her own home, and her own private life, is in the mainstream of life just as much as any married woman. Single women often fear that they have drifted into a backwater and life is hurrying past them; they expend all their energy being absorbed in their own disappointment, and then they wonder why they're unhappy. A positive attitude from an early age would have saved them and set them free to enjoy the exercise of their talents. Why shouldn't we be educated for a life without marriage instead of being conditioned from childhood only for an eventual married existence?

A prominent psychologist not long ago wrote an article pointing out that some people are by their very natures unsuited for marriage. For them to undertake it practically insures the unhappiness of at least two people. In my opinion he was certainly right. I think that women who are very gifted and overly ambitious, those who are extremely self-centered, and those who are dominating and aggressive, should not marry. These women usually have some strong interests of their own, and therefore should make careers of them; they should be emotionally strong enough to face life alone.

As I said earlier, I believe that a woman should have a career or a marriage, but not both. This idea is an old-fashioned one, as my friends often tell me, but there are some old-fashioned ideas that are firmly rooted in common sense. It seems to me that very few women who want to do justice to a career can also do justice to a second career—that of marriage. Marriage is a full-time job if it is treated properly. A husband should have full claim upon his wife's attention; children should never feel that mother is too busy to take notice of them; cooking a meal should be more than a matter of opening a can. A wife who does not give her entire time and energies to these things could cause a marriage to fail, in my opinion, and of necessity she should put family interests before her own personal ambitions, at least until her children are grown up. That doesn't mean she must submerge her own personality and identity—not at all. But being a complete human being involves one's capacity to focus attention on others as well as on one's self.

I sometimes question whether I myself would have been able to make such a sacrifice, even for the husband of my dreams. My principles would have forced me to a choice, but it would have been a hard and bitter one. Could I have ever given up singing? Never have become a radio star or talked to millions of listeners every day? And if I had been married and given up my career, would not my ambitions have fought against my choice and made the adjustment too difficult for me? I am very self-willed by nature, as my adolescent determination to sing showed, and I love my freedom to do what I want when I want to. In spite of my youthful fantasies, I don't think I could have become a good wife. I am very thankful that I made the choice I did.

But I see no reason why a woman who chooses to remain single should forget she is a woman as well as a teacher, nurse, stenographer, professor, entertainer, writer, lawyer or whatever else may be her career. She should take every bit as much interest in her clothes and make-up as a woman who dresses attractively for her husband's return every day. Being unmarried shouldn't be equated with looking like a caricature of the traditional old maid school teacher, although single women too often declare by their unfashionable dress that they couldn't care less. Lack of attention to appearance seems to occur like a contagious disease, I've noticed, among women who live together or work in all-female offices. And it's notorious that the standard of dress at colleges for women is far below that on co-educational campuses. I'm glad to hear that some women's colleges are no longer allowing slacks, shorts, and sneakers, or hair in curlers beneath drab scarves. Women, I believe, should and do dress to please men, but they should dress in the same manner even if men don't happen to be around. (I don't believe that nonsense about women dressing for other women!) In the case of the all-female office, there aren't likely to be men around at any time and dress tends to go daily from bad to worse. Primarily, a woman should dress for her own well-being and self-confidence. I personally can't even think properly if I'm not properly dressed and made up. In the house I have a series of cotton house-dresses I wear in the kitchen and in the mornings, and I never emerge from my bedroom without the proper foundation garments, even if I'm only going marketing. In this way I always feel my best and know I can meet anyone without being at a disadvantage. A nicely dressed, attractively turned out woman shows her self-esteem and self-confidence; a dowdy one seems to be making an apology for her status. And people who continually apologize are boring and pathetic.

If a single woman is well-dressed, attractively made up, and feels reasonably secure there's no reason why

Kate, age three.

Kate during the run of "Honeymoon Lane."

Grandma Hanby, Ted Collins, Kate, and Grandpa Hanby.

May 1, 1931. Kate's first radio broadcast. Her new manager, Ted Collins, is at right. Below: Shortly after she started in radio, Kate had her own musical revue, which opened at the Hippodrome in New York and then toured the country.

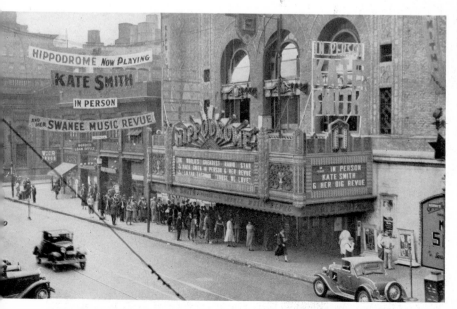

Kate and Ted Collins march with a police escort in a triumphal "Welcome Home" parade in Washington, D.C. Below: The Kate Smith Hour is on the air. Kate, Ted Straeter and his chorus, Ted Collins, Jack Miller, and, with arms extended, André Baruch.

Kate, Bud Abbott and Lou Costello, Irving Berlin, and Ted Collins, with Jack Miller and the band in the background. Below: Backstage before the radio show—Don Ameche, Nancy Kelly, Al Jolson, Ted Collins, and Kate.

Kate visits Pat O'Brien in Hollywood on the set of "The Fighting Sixty-Ninth." Below: Kate and her guests at a combined party and radio broadcast at a performance of the circus at Madison Square Garden in New York.

Eleanor Roosevelt visits Kate on the air.

Kate visits servicemen during the war. She often did her evening hour-long radio show from military installations.

Kate broadcasts a commentator program from her apartment.
Below: *In Dallas on a War Bond tour.*

Brotherhood Week, 1945, with Mayor of New York Fiorello H. LaGuardia. "The National Conference of Christians and Jews presents this citation of Distinguished Merit to Kate Smith, because her radio programs throughout the year embodied the message of understanding and goodwill among all Americans, because she has consistently dedicated herself to the advancement of these ideals."

Relaxed moments at Lake Placid.

With Tyrone Power, Louella Parsons, Ted, and Thomas Mitchell.

At the White House with President Harry Truman.

Kate's mother makes a rare appearance backstage during a *TV* rehearsal. Below: *At home with Freckles.*

*Gertrude Berg (Molly Goldberg) and Benny Goodman were
Kate's guests on her television show. Below: Carlos Montoya,
world-famous flamenco guitarist, was another recent TV guest.*

Jackie Gleason cavorts with Kate at a rehearsal before his guest appearance on her television show, which featured Jackie conducting the orchestra in a selection of his own compositions. Inspired by the title of this book, Jackie has written both words and music of a song composed especially for Kate.

she shouldn't attract as many men friends as she can. There seems to be, in some areas, an assumption that bachelor girls are automatically on the shelf after a certain age, and they make no further attempt to mix socially with men. There's no reason for this. An intelligent woman who is not husband-hunting, but who is interested in having as many friends as possible, should date like any other girl; and she'll often find that men enjoy her well-informed conversation and admire her poise and self-confidence. I have never understood why it is assumed that women, particularly unmarried ones, necessarily prefer the company of women; I thoroughly enjoy the company of my women friends, but I need to meet and talk to men as well. The pleasures of a good conversation depend very largely upon the contrasts and interactions of the masculine and feminine viewpoints. Because a woman is unmarried is no reason why she should be cut off from the stimulation of men's company, although many hostesses seem to think it is. They consider an unmarried woman an embarrassment if they are giving parties, but there's no need to; a single woman who is happy coping with life on her own is not going to be uncomfortable at being unescorted socially. I know of many women who have more men as friends than women. The fact is no slur on their reputations but a tribute to the value placed on their friendship.

A single woman tends perhaps to live too tidy a life, with none of the hurly-burly of youngsters to upset

her plans or scramble over her home; she lives somewhat removed from the realities and bustle of family
life, which require a great flexibility in a woman. If she
can keep in close contact, therefore, with nieces, neph-
ews, or the children of friends, she has solved one of the
great problems of the single life. Adults need a continual
reminder that they haven't been adult all their years.
Children provide us with a constant re-living of our
own growth, discovery and development, and the benefit adults derive from children more than compensates
for the trouble of knowing and understanding them.

A single woman who keeps a vital interest in children
is paying a very pleasant insurance premium against a
lonely old age. When younger people know that they
will always be welcome at an aunt's house and that their
presence will not cause trouble, they will come back
again and again, bringing their vitality with them. The
secret is in keeping flexible. Young people don't want to
feel that visiting an unmarried woman is an excursion
into a dark, enclosed, bitter world, as it so often can be,
and that they mustn't disturb the carefully guarded
routine. The unmarried woman should adapt to the
quicker ways of her young guests, for much of the
world belongs to young people and if you want to enjoy it, keep up with them. I like to think that the youngsters in my family can bounce into my apartment at any
time and find me ready to listen to their latest enthusiasm, whether it's the prospect of a trip to Europe or a

new dress for a prom. I'm always ready to go into the kitchen to make them a snack, no matter what time it is, and even if I have to sleep on a sofa, there's always room for them or for their friends to stay the night. They can teach me more than I can teach them. I do a great deal more listening than talking, and it's good for both of us. I hope "Aunt Kate" is fun for them to be with.

Although the unmarried woman is a woman first and a successful career girl second, she shouldn't suppress her instinct to care for someone or something outside herself. It's impossible to sublimate all instincts in work, and the attempt would do more harm than good. Many unmarried women find themselves looking after an elderly relative even while working; unfortunately, some people regard this as a cross the woman has to bear, instead of the enriching experience it can be. I know single women who daily visit hospital wards where unfortunate children are spending years of their lives. They concentrate on one or more of these children, so often neglected by their own parents, and provide them with love, with gifts, with much-needed attention, and give them a reason to look forward to a tomorrow. These women become, to some of the lonely children, the only "family" they will ever know. It is rewarding to all, to need love and to give love, to care and to be cared for. The greatest gift is, of course, to give of one's self wholeheartedly and without reservation. It is valuable emotional therapy for all, married or unmarried, to give a full measure of devotion to people, to a cause in which we believe, or to the dreams of little children.

Single women have found a multitude of markets for their talents. We hear every day of new and needed projects often born out of one woman's "need" to do for others. I must have told thousands of these stories on my radio and television programs. You don't have to be a Joan of Arc-type heroine and die for a cause. You can live for one, and live excitingly, if you translate that cause into human terms. The world is tremendously big and inviting to a woman not bound by family and home responsibilities. There's no limit to adventure in a world where you are truly willing to participate. There are no boundaries to a "free" woman's universe. There is living to be done; there are undiscovered treasures no married woman has time to search for; vast empires of untapped experiences that can never be known to the woman whose first interest must be the square footage which her husband and children occupy.

There are advantages to being unmarried. This isn't a statement for "old maids whistling in the dark." It's true. Why shouldn't all women admit it along with admitting the advantages of being married? Aloneness is not always loneliness—sometimes it's the priceless privilege of privacy. What married woman wouldn't give a lot for a little of that privacy? The single woman's private world can really be invaded only by invitation. Breathes there a married woman who wouldn't enjoy placing the chain upon her door now and then with a satisfying sigh that, even for a little while, only the persons she wants can cross her threshold?

And what about the lovely feeling of having to make decisions only for yourself and not six times over for husband and family? Surely a married woman will admit that's a rather nice prospect.

It is also perhaps easier for a single woman to find out who she is because there is more time for meditation upon such thoughts. Wouldn't a married woman enjoy the lovely luxury of pondering on her own personality? Of delving into her own ideas and opinions? Wouldn't she find renewed spirit and strength in moments of complete withdrawal uninterrupted by the continuous demands on mother and wife?

So it works both ways, and I believe a great deal of happiness can be found in every circumstance. It isn't only a matter of being married or unmarried. It's more a matter of being complete or incomplete as a human being, of exploring and employing the best that's in us, of adapting and remaining forever flexible, and of resisting being categorized, labeled, pigeon-holed, or price-tagged. You can live a fairly full life in an imperfect world if you have the courage to be "you" and seek out and face all the facts—the facts of a life which is never all you dreamed it would be, but which, nevertheless, is your own life in which you can function well and be important to yourself and others.

Six

I OFTEN wonder whether Ted's Irish ancestry didn't include a leprechaun, for he has so frequently shown instances of uncanny second sight that magic must be involved. He has picked all my songs, and never picked one which wasn't successful. He is able to listen to a song when a composer brings it to him and say immediately whether it will go over with the public or not. He doesn't do it by any reasoning process, but intuitively, almost without a thought.

His management of my career has never shown this magic more clearly than in the way he guided me toward my radio role during the war. If I was ever able to do any good, I am sure it was during those difficult years; I tried to act as a friend to all the millions of women who worried as I did about the progress of the war, and from the volume of mail I received daily I certainly drew a reciprocal strength. But for a radio personality who is merely an unseen voice speaking for a quarter of an hour every day to be accepted as a friend and source of confidence requires more than a little preparation.

We began our commentary program on April 4, 1938. Later in the same year, we launched "God Bless America," on what turned out to be the last November 11, Armistice Day, in a world at peace. Although I loved the song and its simple, effective lyrics, I was afraid it might not be accepted. I worried that it might be considered "too patriotic."

"Look, Kathryn, America needs a song right now. And I honestly think people expect you to come up with one," Ted said.

"Sure, but we'll get called 'flag-wavers,' " I argued.

"Well, if we do, all we have to answer is, 'why not wave the flag?' The flag's a symbol of what the people love about this country. Nothing wrong in waving that flag. I think you're going to be surprised at how well this song will go over. And 'God Bless America' is a lot easier for folks to sing than 'The Star-Spangled Banner.' I think you'll be singing this song so often you'll get tired of it yourself, Kathryn!" he said confidently.

His uncanny judgment of the mood of the public was right again. Irving Berlin's "God Bless America" became "my" song, just as "When the Moon Comes Over the Mountain" was "my" song. When I first sang it, Mr. Berlin announced that any profits from its performance would go to the Boy Scouts of America, in a fund to be administered by Herbert Bayard Swope, Gene Tunney, and Theodore Roosevelt, Jr.

The song caught on like wild-fire. Within a few months movements began to spring up to replace "The Star-Spangled Banner" with "God Bless America" as the national anthem. We never anticipated nor wanted that. In spite of the fact that Irving Berlin's song is much easier to sing, it doesn't have the historical dignity of "The Star-Spangled Banner," and consequently these efforts became very embarrassing to us. People began to write me asking whether they should stand up when "God Bless America" was sung, and I devoted several spots on my noontime program to an emphatic denial of the appropriateness of any such suggestion. Finally the discussion reached Congress, where there was a demand for a bill that would make the song the new national anthem. At this point Ted went to Washington himself to ask that this not be done.

During the presidential primaries of 1940, I received a request from the Democratic National Committee to sing "God Bless America" at the convention before the speeches. Ted looked at the letter with its elaborate heading and pursed his mouth.

"No, Kathryn, not unless the Republicans ask you too," he said, giving the letter back to me. " 'God Bless

America' has no political affiliation. That song's for all Americans and so is your voice."

By the time the United States entered the war, a number of factors, including "God Bless America," had combined to define my role for the listening public. Throughout 1940 and 1941, when America was watching the war in Europe with fear, worrying whether we would be able to stay out of it, I tried to answer the continual question women would ask me in their letters: "What can I do?" My reply was "You can pray." I told them to read, to listen, to keep informed, and to strengthen their family life. Often I talked of other things—of the eternal values, the wonders of nature and the laughter of children, the moral fiber our history wove for us. I spoke of acts of heroism and self-sacrifice which were in the news and often gave awards to people who performed them—people who ordinarily never made headlines. I spoke to women of their importance as homemakers and mothers and stressed the values of ordinary tasks well done every day.

My preference for such subjects made my noon program into an interval of comfort and cheerfulness for my audience. My views were simple and perhaps even old-fashioned. I wanted to be an anchor of wholesome wisdom on which women felt they could depend.

This image was brilliantly projected by Ted, who wrote many of my scripts, and supervised all of them after they were written. He gave them his characteristic touch. Whenever we discussed a topic for the noon program, he always managed to put into words the exact point of view I had in my own mind. I would mention that I thought we ought to speak about *Little Women* on the birthday of Louisa May Alcott, for example, and within an hour he would produce a tribute expressed precisely the way I wanted it expressed. There is between us an uncanny, almost telepathic, mental sympathy.

From the day of Pearl Harbor onward, the commentary programs were directed to one end—victory. The home front was my natural field, and I felt I wanted to fight there for all the values in which I believed. Faith in the outcome was the first and most important message I had. Ted never once allowed any suggestion to enter my scripts that the war would end in anything but victory for the Allies.

The war years were a period of hard work for both of us. We had not only the five noon programs every week, but the weekly hour-long program, and then an increasing number of appearances for the USO in camps throughout the United States as well. Ted was given a job by the government involving additional broadcasts; in 1942 he often made as many as fourteen broadcasts a week.

One day in August, 1943, Ted entered the office at 1819 Broadway where I was reading through some of the mail the staff had set aside for my personal attention. Since the beginning of the war we had closed the house at Lake Placid and no longer got out of the city for the summer; because gas was rationed, I had given up my car as well.

Ted flung his straw hat on to a chair and said, "I'll be glad when the war's over and we can be cool in the summer again. Anyone who can stand August in New York ought to be able to win a war single-handed." He sat down and looked at what I was doing.

"Forget the mail, Kathryn. We've got a bigger job to get ready for, now. Third War Bond Drive."

"Well, it's about time," I answered, pushing the letters aside. "We haven't done anything about war bonds since last October. What's the idea for this one?"

"I've just been talking to the CBS boys. They're going to put you on a nation-wide hook-up this time, not just New York or Washington. You're going to do a marathon—you know, about eighteen hours at the microphone, spots every few minutes throughout the day."

"Like the first two we did," I said.

"Yes, but I want this to be much better. I want to spend a lot of time choosing themes for this one so that we make a specific effect. I want some real organization in it. That's why I've started so far in advance—we're not going to do it until September twenty-first."

"What's the matter—afraid we won't better our record?"

"No, no, we'll do that. I just want to see how efficient we can be in using every part of your appeal. The public has a picture of you as a sincere, generous patriot. I'd like to see just how far we can use this to raise as much money as possible. Your position in radio is unique. Half the women in America drop everything to listen to you every day. They'd probably make any sacrifice you asked them to. Why shouldn't we use this power you have for a good cause in a time of crisis?"

"I agree with you, Ted. I'm just glad it's a good cause."

"Don't worry, Kathryn, you'll never do anything against your conscience. Now, here's what I want you to do during the next few weeks: think up, read, or find in your mail any stories of sacrifice you think we could use as examples on September twenty-first. You know—a woman who so much wants to bring her son home from the war that she sells a family heirloom to raise money to buy bonds. That kind of thing. You're going to appeal primarily to women, so you're a better judge than I am of the kind of stories that'll move them," he smiled.

"All right. I guess this means you'll cut down your sleep from four hours a night to three, now, Ted."

He laughed and picked up his hat. "There'll be plenty of time to sleep when the war is over."

About three weeks before the drive was due to take place on September 21, Ted called a conference of the three writers on the Kated staff to brief them. He asked them all to bring forward any ideas they might have for themes, whether they seemed useful or not at first glance. There was a silence and then a girl who had been with us from the beginning and who had worked her way up from secretary to scriptwriter, spoke.

"As I see it, Ted, the first and most important theme we must stress is the sacrifice our men overseas are making. We ought to balance this against the sacrifice we at home are making by buying bonds. Something like: 'There's a boy lying wounded on a field in Italy. He's sacrificed his health. What are you giving that's worth as much?' We could find lots of stories of this kind," she said.

"That's what we want. Now why don't you consider yourself responsible for working up the sacrifice theme? There are going to be well over sixty broadcasts during the day, so you'll need to get a large number of stories," said Ted, with an encouraging smile at the girl.

"Wait a minute—there's more than one kind of sacrifice we can use," said another girl, very slim and well-dressed. "I was thinking of the sacrifice of mothers at home: 'What are you doing to equal the sacrifice this woman is making in giving her only son to be killed?' And what about the sacrifice of Kate herself?"

I broke in with a laugh. "It isn't much of a sacrifice to just sit in front of a microphone and do what you like best all day—and I like talking best!"

"No, Kathryn, maybe you don't think it's a sacrifice, but we've got to impress on the listeners that you're giving time and trouble and your voice to the cause," said Ted patiently.

"Yes, but don't insist too much. Just let me say once or twice that I've been there for so many hours and I'm going to be there until two o'clock in the morning, and that's all."

"There you are—she's written that bit for you!" said Ted, turning to the writer. "By the way, Kathryn, how would you like to be photographed at the end of the marathon, collapsing, with a nurse and doctor in attendance? Stretchers, bottles of medicine and all!"

I bridled at first and then laughed. "You can't be serious. I took twenty-four hours of it last year and felt better with each hour, so I'm certainly not going to faint under eighteen hours. Whose idea was this anyway?"

"It was the publicity department of CBS that suggested it," said Ted, laughing with me. "Other stars who've been doing marathons apparently have been feeling the strain pretty badly around about midnight, so the publicity boys thought they'd line up a doctor and nurse for you, too."

"Other stars don't have my weight behind them," I said. "And I'd hate to have a doctor and nurse waste their time waiting for me to faint with exhaustion. Tell 'em they'll have to think up something better than that, Ted."

"Aw, they won't need any fancy publicity ideas when they see the total we come up with," said Ted.

Our third writer, a crew-cut young man with a rather solemn face, who had been scribbling notes on his pad throughout the banter, now cleared his throat and said, "Look, Ted, why don't we analyze what war bonds are for and see what we can get out of that? At this point in the war, they aren't for buying material. In fact, that little book of instructions to sellers of bonds says you aren't to say the money will go for guns, because everybody knows better than that now."

"Go on," said Ted, listening with an enigmatic expression.

"Here we are, our men are in Italy and pushing up into Europe. It's only a matter of time until a second front is established. Roosevelt has already started considering plans for demobilization after the end of the war. So what are we raising war bonds for?"

Our former secretary looked puzzled. "I hadn't thought of that," she said.

The young man went on. "The idea of putting money in bonds now is to get it out of circulation and to stop inflation. There hasn't been enough production of goods because factories have been producing armaments, and consequently people have more money to spend than goods to buy. Naturally, prices will go up in such circumstances, but they won't if money is salted away in war bonds. Now why shouldn't we use this theme? Why not something like—cooperate with your government now and enjoy your savings when there's something to spend them on?"

"Seems like a good idea," said the slim girl. "There are two good themes there—stop inflation is one and invest for your future is another." They all looked at Ted for his approval. He stood up and walked to the window before turning and shaking his head.

"No, kids, that won't do. It's the wrong attitude for Kate. Kate's appeal is essentially emotional and those themes require too much thinking. You can't make women buy bonds by giving them reasons. You've got to play on their feelings. That's too cold, too logical."

"But it's true, Ted. How are you going to ignore it? What are you going to tell them they're buying bonds for?" the writer persisted.

"We'll leave that as vague as we can. We'll say something like: 'Buy a bond to bring your boy home. Buy a bond to end the war.' Something emotional."

"Sure, we can do that," said the man, "but will it be enough?"

"It will if you make the sacrifice story vivid enough. You can work on their feelings so much that they won't care where the money's going as long as they can buy a bond and feel they're doing something. And I haven't forgotten the inflation business, either. I'm thinking of using it in Kate's regular noon broadcasts—but I'm going to make it emotional, too."

"How are you going to do that?" asked the former secretary.

"Appeal to people not to spend because if they do they'll be buying another depression. Bring back memories they wish they didn't have of the early nineteen thirties," he answered.

"Okay," said the solemn young man, "so we can't use the inflation theme. But I've got a few more here. What about playing on the competitive spirit? 'Help Kate Smith to make this the biggest, best, most colossal bond drive ever.' "

"Sure, that's good," replied Ted. "But there's more than one theme there. There's the personal idea that it's Kate's drive and she needs help to beat out the other marathoners. Then there's the feeling that we're all pulling together—'if you help, we can all win'—that sort of angle. There's also the family side of it—'let's get together to bring back a son,' and so on. You look after all those, will you? And see how many more angles you can figure out to do with competition and cooperation."

"By the way, Ted," I asked, "how are we taking orders this time? I don't have to answer the telephone, do I?"

"No, we could only have you answering personally when we were on in New York City alone. This time we're getting numbers of extra telephones put in at the CBS stations and hiring girls temporarily to answer them and take orders. That reminds me," he said, turning to Minnie, who was taking notes during the meeting, "Minnie, make a note that I want a mimeographed sheet given to each of those girls. I want to ask them to report to the studio if anybody they take an order from has an interesting story."

"You mean, so that we can add them in as the marathon goes along?" I asked.

"Yes. I'd like to get a sort of give-and-take feeling with the listeners. I'll bet some will even buy just to hear their own case mentioned."

"That's another thing I thought we ought to use," said the young man. "We ought to stress how easy it is to buy your bond. You don't have to go to a bank or stand in line—all you have to do is reach for the phone and give your name and address."

"Fine, that's yours too. And we've got to have a slogan to be repeated at the end of each spot," said Ted. "Something which really gets at them so that they wait for it to come and can't switch off until it does."

"Something like, 'Won't you buy a bond, please?'" asked the slim girl.

"That's the idea. Now, any more ideas for themes? Doesn't matter—we've got enough for a week's marathon as it is. I'd like all of you to go off and write a series of spots, using your own particular themes and putting everything you've got into them. Kate will give you some ideas herself, won't you, Kathryn? She's been looking for stories ever since we knew about this drive. Then, I'd like to have all your stuff—and make it enough for at least seventy two-minute spots—a week before the date, so I can start editing and polishing and we've got time for re-writing."

"What are you going to do, Ted—make each spot deal with one theme, or mix them?" asked the solemn young man.

"Don't know yet. Might do one or the other, or both.

But I want plenty so that we can vary things as we go along. And I'd also like you all to be on call on September twenty-first, to deal with anything that might come up."

There was an air of tenseness and excitement in the studio when we arrived there shortly after 5:30 on the morning of September 21. This was going to be our first nation-wide effort, and we were expecting to raise well over twenty million dollars. Our previous local marathons had raised one million dollars in pledges in New York and two million in Washington, but now, as Ted said, we were into the big league. On the desk beside the microphone was a pile of scripts; some of them I had read, but most of them had come fresh from the typist after Ted finished editing and revising them. Each had a time on it: the first was 8:00, then 8:15, and so on throughout the day.

Ted put his hand on them as he gave me his last few words of advice. "We'll pretty much follow these as they are until after the noon broadcast, Kathryn," he said. "There won't be too much coming in until then. We've got to wait until the repetition of the appeal has had time to work on people. Then afterward I doubt if we'll follow them much. Maybe we'll use the main story in each one and then fill in with reports on totals from all over the country and stories the phone girls get."

"I like the story for the noon broadcast very much, by the way," I said. "Did you write it all?"

"No, I just touched up what the girl had written. Certainly was an inspiration she had there. That's one of the spots where I want you to give all you've got. I'd like you to feel a sort of shape to the marathon as we go along, making climaxes in the middle of the morning, at noon, and at six o'clock when the men are home from work. We've spaced the best stories that way—you'll see."

I sat down before the microphone and waited for the signal to go on the air. For one moment I remembered my first experience of this sort, when I had been a girl watching for that red light to go on for the very first time. I smiled to myself. The thought of having over twelve years before a microphone since that day helped me to feel confident that this was going to be one of my best days on radio. The announcer told the audience that this was CBS Bond Day and I was going to broadcast appeals for bonds throughout the day. Then I began my first appeal, telling listeners that the total of pledges would be posted on my studio wall under the clock.

"Right now," I read into the microphone, "there's nothing up there. It's a complete blank. This is the beginning. I hope to watch the figures on the wall grow from two to three to four, to five and six figures, until we reach well over twenty million dollars to help end this war. So, folks, won't you please buy a bond? All you have to do is pick up your telephone and dial the number your local announcer will give you. Girls are standing by at the telephones waiting to take your name and address. It's so easy—and it means so much. Won't you please buy a bond now?"

As soon as we were off the air, a feeling of relief swept over us. It was on; we had begun. We sent out at once for doughnuts and coffee, knowing that we probably wouldn't be able to eat them until after the next spot was done.

A couple of hours passed. News of bond sales began to come in, and we put up the figures on the wall. Ted told me not to report them yet, but to wait until they were really spectacular.

I began to feel that I wasn't alone behind a microphone, but was part of a great movement of people all trying their utmost to find enough money to buy another bond. I was told afterward that many women listened to my every broadcast, hoping that I would be able to raise a record number of bonds, but even while the marathon was on I could feel their sympathy urging me on. It came in the stories the girls heard over the telephone, in the mounting totals reported from towns and cities across the country, in the tense atmosphere of the studio as Ted and the writers worked to get the last drop of appeal from the latest reports.

At noontime, when I did my regular broadcast, I devoted it all to a long appeal for bond pledges. Since I had nearly fifteen minutes instead of one or two as in the other spots, there was an opportunity to develop a theme at length. I used the story I had liked so much when I first read it, for it expressed all I deeply believed in:

"All over America, autumn is dancing over the hills and plains, tapping out the rhythm of the changing season. All over America, the same dear familiar beauty is spread, as we go about our work and our play. It's football time and school time and harvest time, time of State Fairs and the opening of new plays, time for shopping for winter clothes, time for looking forward to Thanksgiving and Christmas. We are at war, we're working harder, we're missing many dear ones, but otherwise our busy, beautiful world is the same. No bombs pierce the peaceful silence of our night, no smoke hides the glory of our sunsets, no alien hands plunder our possessions or send us off to prison camps in a life that is worse than death.

"But somewhere in the mud and the grime and noise of the battlefront a young man in khaki lies sprawled on unfamiliar earth. He lies very still and in his eyes there is untold agony. The guns of the enemy have gotten him, and as his comrades plunge forward into the black hell of war, he waits for the stretcher-bearers. He lies very still now. Six feet of strong, husky, American manhood, blond hair tangled with dust and blackened with smoke, brave body stained with blood. He's twenty-one years old and for fourteen months that seem like centuries, he's been in the thick of battle a long way from home. He was just an average American kid, came from a little town like any other American town—a white

143

church on a hill, a fishing stream winding through the valley, a town hall and a high school, and a job in the drug-store on Main Street. He used to play football and basketball and take girls to dances on Saturday night. He belonged to the village library and sang in the church choir and went to the movies over at the Palace. He liked life in his town; liked having breakfast in the kitchen, with his Mom frying his eggs and pouring his morning coffee. He liked seeing her there, her cheeks rosy, her stout form enveloped in a gingham apron. He liked Sis and the steadfast look in her eyes when she said: 'I pledge allegiance to the flag of the United States.' He liked to hear Dad talk politics and the way he pounded his work-worn fist on the table and said: 'No matter how you look at it, there is no substitute for democracy.' He liked racing around in his old Ford, crowding it with his gang, and slipping nickels in juke boxes and dancing to songs like the 'Hut Sut Song,' 'Rose O'Day' and 'I Don't Want To Set the World on Fire.'

"No, he didn't want to set the world on fire. He wanted to live and work and love and get married. He wanted always to be able to watch the sun go down behind those hills of home and walk in the familiar ways all Americans love. He wanted Thanksgiving and Christmas and trees aglitter with lights and ice-skating on the pond, and to join his lusty voice with those of his friends singing 'Silent Night, Holy Night,' and sometimes, when the mood was right, harmonizing that

144

perennial favorite, 'Sweet Adeline.' That's all he wanted, this boy who now lies very still on the field of battle. There was just one more thing, a thing he didn't think about very often, but it was there all right, wrapped close and warm in his heart, that thing called love of country. He wanted freedom and liberty and the kind of a land America had been since its hardy beginnings. That's why he cheerfully turned his back upon all the things he loved, because he was willing and eager to fight and die for their preservation."

There were tears on my cheek as I read, and I had to choke back a sob before I could continue:

"He's lying wounded on a battlefield now. He doesn't want to be there. He wants to be home, safe in his comfortable, clean white bed. He doesn't want to die—nobody wants to die. He didn't like to fight and shoot and kill. No decent human being enjoys those things. But he went right ahead for you and for me and for millions of Americans, who are at this moment living safe, happy, comfortable lives, making more money than they've ever made before, perhaps; eating plenty, living the good easy American life every one of us prefers. Why should he be there on that blood-stained battlefield? Why should he, and thousands upon thousands of our youth, be carrying the burden? Why in God's name should he lay down his precious life on the altar of freedom while we go our accustomed ways in comfort and safety? Is there any way we can repay him? Is there any way we can even up the score, and repay him for even a tiny portion of his sacrifice? Is there any way we can get this ghastly war over more quickly for him and for his comrades-in-arms?

"You all know the answer—back the attack! Buy bonds and more bonds, not only as a good investment, not only as a gesture of patriotism, but because you're everlastingly grateful, because you're down on your knees thanking your Creator that we have Americans fighting for freedom, fighting for victory. Because you can never possibly do enough or give enough or sacrifice enough or buy enough to pay the colossal debt we owe to those who stand between us and the enemy. They're standing there, all right, and they're pushing the enemy back on every front. Back the attack with every dollar, every penny you can spare! And be thankful that you're lending your money instead of laying down your life in the cause of victory and peace. Won't you please buy a bond, now?"

I paused, my voice almost breaking, and then finished: "You'll be hearing from me for the next fourteen hours."

There was silence in the studio as I stopped speaking. I wiped my face where the tears had stained it. Ted looked across at me with an encouraging smile, and we all realized at that moment, as never before, the solemnity of what we were undertaking. I was glad that there was to be quite a long interval before the next spot, so that I could collect my thoughts and rest a little.

As the afternoon went on, stories kept coming in: a woman had pawned her wedding ring to buy bonds, two little girls had broken their piggy bank and just raised enough between them to buy a bond, a grandmother bought a bond with the money she had intended for a sumptuous layette for her new grandchild. Sometimes we scrapped the prepared scripts altogether and replaced them with these stories and reports of our mounting total. It was up to nearly ten million dollars by about four o'clock.

At about this time I began to feel very tired, but I knew I was only getting my second wind and would recover in an hour or two. I found my voice getting harsh and had to sip water before each broadcast, and I had a tendency to yawn and want to put my head down when each spot ended. It was difficult to get a real rest between the appeals because by the time I relaxed completely I had to get back to the microphone. But there was no question of my collapsing of exhaustion; by the time six o'clock came around and we were ready for another big appeal, I had completely recovered. I could have gone on for another day after that. And the ever-increasing figure on the wall opposite me would have kept me going in any condition.

We devoted the six o'clock appeal to the competitive aspects of the marathon. I put into my voice everything I usually use when cheering on a football team, to get people to help me send the drive over the top.

"We can do this together, you and I," I said, "if you

only telephone that pledge in now. We can all make this the biggest bond drive of all time. Millions of dollars have already been pledged, but there are still millions more that could be helping to swell the total. Won't you please buy a bond now?"

Ted smiled as he slipped a script to me just before eight o'clock at night. "This will tell us whether we've still got friends," he said.

I read: "Hello everybody, this is Kate Smith again, appealing to you to make this CBS War Bond Drive a real record. You've heard me say over and over again today—won't you please buy a bond? You're probably sick and tired of the sound of my voice asking that question, but it's still an important one and I still have to go on asking it. I don't like to keep pestering you to buy a bond, but the sooner you do it, the sooner I'll stop. You see, this is something I firmly believe in and I'm going to keep on repeating it, even at the risk of boring you; will you, as an American, help to back the attack, help to bring our American boys back home, by buying a bond now? Even if you've bought bonds before—or bought them earlier today—buy another one now. And I'll be back again in a few minutes to make another appeal to you."

We passed the twenty million dollar mark before midnight, and the atmosphere in the studio became much lighter. Now we were going to press for more just to see how much we could raise. Ted was watching the reports of the pledges very closely; he began to write in comments on each city so that there was something of the excitement of the end of a race about the last couple of hours. Who would come out first? More and more it looked as if Los Angeles was giving us the most pledges, although New York was close behind. Ted was amazed at this, since at that time New York's population was very much larger than that of Los Angeles; the years since the war have narrowed the gap. Finally, at about 12:45, he called a hurried conference with the writers and the studio manager.

"Look, I think we can get some extra pledges by playing on the pride of the New Yorkers. I'd like to close down the country-wide circuit at two o'clock and go on for an hour in New York alone to give them a chance to catch up. They'll be furious that L.A. is ahead, and we should get another half million." Orders went out by long-distance telephone to the stations, and writers began on last-minute scripts.

At two o'clock, when the figure on the wall stood at over thirty million dollars, Ted said, "Move over, Kathryn, this is my turn. You're not a New Yorker. Besides, a fresh voice will give them that last boost."

So he took my place and said, "This is Ted Collins speaking to you from New York. In the mammoth War Bond Drive conducted by Kate Smith and just concluded, the city of Los Angeles has bought more war bonds than the people of New York. Now I'm a New Yorker myself, and it makes me feel kind of sad to see the old home town being outdone. So we're going to continue the war bond drive here in New York for one more hour, giving New Yorkers a chance to catch up with Los Angeles."

Then he handed the microphone back to me for one last hour. And when we finally closed down, we had raised thirty-nine million dollars in bonds.

But Ted was not satisfied that we had done all we possibly could. He kept talking about it in the weeks that followed. He kept saying, "There's something missing somewhere. I keep hearing people in the streets talking about it and I'm trying to pick up clues so that next time we can raise three times as much."

He didn't have to wait very long for us to get another opportunity, for CBS scheduled its fourth marathon for me on February 1, 1944. This was to be a twenty-four-hour drive, which in itself meant that we would increase the amount raised. I asked Ted what else we could do.

"Well, I think I've hit on something we forgot last time—an appeal to the men, directly to them, instead of almost exclusively to women."

"I think that'll be rather tough," I said, "because I know very well that my following is largely female. You said yourself last time that the sort of arguments that appeal to men, you know, investments and so on, aren't my style."

"Yes, but there's a way to get around that. I'm going to write a special bit myself for you, and you can bet now that the total will shoot up. After all, in most households it's the husband who controls the spending of the large amounts that bonds cost. If we can get the men to phone in, we'll go above the hundred-million-dollar mark in twenty-four hours.

When six o'clock in the evening came 'round on February 1, the situation was much the same as it had been during the third drive. We used different stories, of course, but the themes were essentially the same. Now I noticed that I had a quarter of an hour scheduled for me instead of only two minutes, and Ted said to me as we went into it, "Here's where we branch off and get into the real money."

The script he had written for me was a masterpiece. It converted my emotional appeal from the feminine to the masculine audience, while still retaining its essential character. I addressed myself directly to the men, and said first of all that I knew many people had complained that my appeals were full of "emotionalism."

"Yes, that's what they say, these wise people who only know the world of dollars and cents. That's what they say. They are the people who say that bond-buying is a matter of hard-headed thinking and budgeting, not something to be undertaken on the spur of the moment at the sound of a sentimental appeal. But I don't believe it, gentlemen. I think they lie, these people who think our American businessmen don't like emotionalism, don't harbor sentiment in their hearts. Because these

American men, who are working at home and doing an essential job, are the fathers of the sons for whom I'm working today.

"They are the fathers of the splendid boys who have gone into battle because of ideals and sentiment and love of country. They went for the same motives that sent you, their dads, to war in nineteen-seventeen. Nobody can tell me that you, their fathers here at home, aren't bursting with pride. Nobody can tell me that you can sit down coolly and separate sentiment—or emotionalism, if you want to call it that—from bond-buying. How about it, Mr. America? Are you going to count the cost, and do planned bookkeeping, when our kids overseas have some accounts of their own to balance—in blood? Will you listen to your heart, now?"

From then until eight o'clock the next morning when the drive closed, I continued this appeal to the men among my listeners. Ted had worked out many variations on the theme; I think he had written them on the basis of what would move him, personally.

The men were convinced, I'm sure, for when the fourth war bond drive closed, we had raised a hundred and ten million dollars in pledges.

Seven

IT I S and always has been my belief that an entertainer should in his public performance keep himself out of any controversy, political or otherwise, and should also refrain from using his power over the public to further any private cause he may support as an individual. I also believe that an entertainer, because he is so much in the public eye, should be a person whom the public can admire; his sincerity and honesty in his work should be a model for young people.

In view of these convictions, I have always examined closely the motives of any group for which I am asked to raise money. The experience with war bonds taught me what a power I can have over an audience. It is a tremendous responsibility. This power sometimes frightens me. Sitting at home not long after the third marathon, I thought about it.

Because of my voice, speaking words which had been carefully chosen, women had used money they had set aside for other purposes to buy war bonds. When the emotional impact of my words died, would they regret what they had done? Would their husbands call them weak and be angry? Could I, in fact, have been spreading more unhappiness than happiness by employing my influence?

What I stood for was clear in the minds of the people whom I had persuaded to buy bonds; to them, therefore, almost any cause I endorsed would be praiseworthy. They would not stop to question the value of the cause, just as they did not stop to reason out the effects of their using their money to buy war bonds. It is frightening to consider what an unscrupulous person in my position could do in a society like ours. All I had done was to persuade people to part with their money, but it is within the realm of possibility that—had I wanted to, had I been the tool of a political party—I could have persuaded them to part with their votes, and therefore their liberty.

Luckily, the purchasing of war bonds for any reason at all, whether to help the men in the army or to fight inflation, was calculated to aid the welfare of everybody in America; the use of the techniques of mass persuasion was therefore justified. I have tried to follow my principles in everything I have asked people to do on my program—and that even extends to the products I advertise. I have personally believed in every product I have ever advertised—that is, until one of my recent series of television shows, the commercials for which, in my opinion, violated many principles of good taste.

Whenever a sponsor launched a new product, or asked me to advertise something I had not previously recommended, Ted and I would go down to the company's testing kitchens and sample the product. Sometimes I even baked a cake right there, and then was photographed eating it. The photographs were the ruin of my good intentions, for they seemed to need so many shots that often a complete cake was used before they were satisfied. Then cake mixes and ingredients were given me to try at home before I advertised them, and that meant more cake, more puddings, more desserts.

Every Friday evening when we were putting on the hour-long show at the Columbia Playhouse, General Foods would deliver at least one cake to my dressing room in the theater. After fifteen years of this, it's hardly surprising that I was no lightweight.

Hard work in the studio was another contributing factor, particularly when we started in television in 1950. When a group of actors and technicians are working together, eating seems to go on all day long; someone has a break and says he'll go out and get coffee and doughnuts and would anyone else like some? Of course everyone would, and this goes on and on. Because of my preoccupation with sweet things for General Foods, I developed a taste for cakes and pies and desserts. Whenever I took a snack, it invariably consisted of something sweet with coffee. Ice cream was also my undoing, and six chocolate milk shakes in a row were nothing to me at one time.

So for many years I could blame my extra weight to a large extent on the sincerity of my advertising! When it became obvious in 1957 that I was endangering my health by carrying so much weight, I was faced with the problem of getting rid of the desire to eat sweets. It was a task which took months—and no food company as sponsor!

You might have thought that the war years with their rationing and shortages would have automatically made overeating difficult, but unfortunately my frequent visits to entertain at camps for the USO took care of that. While civilians were economizing in every direction, the army quite naturally had abundant supplies of everything; the soldiers usually thought they would show their gratitude for my singing by helping me out with food.

Ted and I would be eating dinner with the camp commander and his officers, when one of them would lean confidentially toward me.

"By the way, Miss Smith," he would ask in a low voice, "I suppose you find coffee hard to get?"

"Why, yes, it is tough," I would answer, "particularly since I drink so much of it."

"Well, then, I'll see what I can do about letting you have a case of ours," he'd say, straightening up and turning to the general conversation.

In some camps things were obviously stricter and this conversation did not take place. But then usually, before or after the show, I would find the mess sergeant wanting to talk to me backstage.

"Miss Smith, look in your car when you get out of the camp. The commanding officer's a bit tight here, but we can spare it for you."

And there would be a case—or even two—of the best coffee on the back seat.

Eventually this kindness began to get very embarrassing. I appreciated the intention but felt it should not have occurred. Soon I found a way to say no.

"Well, thank you, I don't drink so much coffee now—I've gone off it a bit."

"Do you have enough Corn Flakes then, Miss Smith?"

And the Corn Flakes came pouring in. The Smith and Collins families ate Corn Flakes for breakfast, supper, and snacks, and had sweets made of Corn Flakes and cakes made of Corn Flakes. The process was repeated with sugar and went on down the list of scarce commodities. The armed forces apparently felt a good singer, like an army, needs a full stomach.

I haven't much of a head for languages. I wish I did. I've never mastered another language but I was able to pick up a certain amount of Yiddish from Jews and non-Jews in show business. The colorful and descriptive words and phrases are used by many. And Yiddish is the language of a people who have lived in many lands, a link precious to Jews of East European backgrounds, as well as being a language of particular interest to entertainers for its heritage of the Yiddish theater. Consequently I was delighted to be asked to sing at a charity concert to benefit a Yiddish theater on the East side of New York.

I felt it would be an appropriate gesture to learn a little of the language myself to identify with the cause. I got Molly Picon, a famous actress in the Yiddish theater, to come to my apartment a few evenings before the performance. Together we worked out a little speech and she taught me exactly how to say it. We rehearsed over and over again until I sounded as if I understood what the words meant apart from this context. I also sang a Yiddish song, and Molly made me sing the phrases repeatedly, so that I got the stresses in the right places and the right vowel sounds came easily to me.

The concert took place at the theater itself, which was full of people of many national origins united in their understanding of Yiddish, and a surprisingly large number of gentiles who admired the spirit of the Yiddish theater. I came on stage and delivered my carefully learned speech before I sang. The audience applauded wildly, as much from astonishment as pleasure. They didn't know Kate Smith spoke Yiddish! Then I went on to sing my song in Yiddish as a finale to my performance of English songs.

After the show, a number of people crowded around me at a reception backstage. I saw Molly Picon, who had taught me my speech, and I waved to her. But I was delayed in getting to her by the number of people who all wished to speak to me—in Yiddish. I watched their faces and their swiftly-moving lips. Every so often I understood a word and vigorously nodded my head. Then I would answer as well as I could from what I had learned; sentiments from my little speech would be appropriate, I thought, plus a few affirmatives and expressions of thanks. I did notice one or two odd looks come over the faces of the people I spoke to, but I put it down to my poor grammar. In any case, the atmosphere was cordial enough to forgive a small slip. I was beaming by the time I managed to get through to see Molly. To my surprise she was choking with laughter.

"What's the matter?" I asked.

"It's all right, Kate, you did splendidly, except that all the time you were saying 'yes' when you should have been saying 'no!' "

Before the war, we took many trips across country, usually traveling by train to Chicago and then striking southwest toward Hollywood, where we celebrated premieres of a number of movies. On one of these trips, Jeannette and Ted Collins and I decided to leave the train at Phoenix, Arizona, and go by car across the desert to Los Angeles. We wanted to go at a more leisurely pace and stop at towns which were not on the railroad track.

One morning we set out from the hotel in a hired car and traveled for some miles over dusty roads, not seeing a car or a human being for long stretches. Ted said he'd hate to get stuck on such a road, because it might be hours before help came along.

Shortly afterward we decided we'd better get gas at the next station, since distances between stations were so long we didn't dare risk running out. We pulled into a forlorn yard where two gas pumps shimmered in the sunshine; there was a shack behind them, and another shack to one side, where no doubt the man who owned the station lived. There was nothing else but sand for miles on every side.

No one came out of the shack for some minutes, so Ted looked at his wallet while waiting. When the man came up, Ted said to him, "Have you got change for a twenty-dollar bill?"

"Nope." The man, dressed in jeans and a dirty shirt, shook his head, not changing the expression of resignation on his face. "Not many autos come through here in a day," he offered as an explanation.

Ted turned to Jeannette and myself, but it was one of those curious situations where none of us had any change. I too had a twenty-dollar bill, never dreaming that I would hit somewhere where it couldn't be changed. All Jeannette had was fifty cents in change.

"Will you take a check, then, for gas?" asked Ted.

The man shook his head again. "Nope. I've had too many checks with nothing behind them," he said.

"How far to the next gas station?" asked Ted.

"About seventy miles down the road," answered the man, with his air of detachment.

"Well, we haven't got enough gas to get there," said Ted. "Look, you can trust our checks. I can give you identification."

"No good, mister. Never can tell with you people from the East."

We looked at each other and wondered what to do. I suggested to Ted that he tell the man who we were.

"Look, you can trust us. We'll give you a check, or could you give us the gas on credit and let us send you the money from Los Angeles? The lady here's Kate Smith, and I'm Ted Collins. We've got to get to L.A. as soon as possible because we're going to do a broadcast there."

The man looked at me with disbelief; his face clearly said that if I was Kate Smith, he was the King of Siam.

"I don't care who you are and who the lady is, mister. I've got a living to make and I can't go giving gas to strangers, especially with big cars like yours. It'd take about fifteen gallons, by the look of it. Sorry, can't help you."

He turned and walked into the shack, closing the door to keep out the growing heat.

"Well, now what are we going to do?" I asked, without much hope of getting a constructive answer.

"There isn't much to do but wait," said Ted. "Something's bound to come through here before nightfall. There's no point in our trying to leave, because we'll run out of gas before we get to the next station. And we can't go back either. So you'd better get used to it, ladies."

We sat there, completely deflated. The door of the shack remained closed. Ted said the man had probably gone back to sleep, since there wasn't much else he could do. The heat, which had not been too hard to bear when the car was moving and creating a breeze, now became stifling. Even with sunglasses on, the glare from the sand hurt our eyes. We tried getting out and walking around, but it was hotter in the full light of the sun than it was even in the closed car. Time went by, and we began to get thirsty. We realized that water was at a premium in this part of the country because along the road there were advertisements reminding you to get your water-bottles filled for a small charge. There was of course no water in the gas station, and we began to wish we had a water-bottle.

For nearly three hours we sat there, watching the glaring road for some sign of an approaching car. We felt that to live there as the garage man did must be very hard on the nerves, since the loneliness had begun to oppress us in only a matter of hours. We wondered why he lived there alone, or whether he just came out there for a certain number of days a week and was then replaced by someone else. In spite of our plight, we sympathized with him; it was a hard way to earn a living and he must have had to watch each penny.

We had eaten all the candy bars we had with us in our first hour, and were beginning to get very hungry as well as thirsty and irritable, when we saw at last some movement at the end of the road. Slowly a vehicle came into view, and we saw that it was an army truck. Never had such a vehicle seemed so welcome. We all got out of the car as it approached, and Ted stood in the middle of the road and waved his arms. The truck halted and Ted jumped on the running board to explain our predicament.

The driver looked through a panel cut in the back of the cabin and called to the men sitting in the back.

"Who's got change for a twenty-dollar bill for Kate Smith?" he yelled.

A man jumped out of the back and was followed by several others. When they saw me, they began searching in their pockets and between them they made change. Then one came up to me and said, "Say, Miss Smith, how about an autograph for my wife? She listens to your program every day."

So, standing on that dusty road, I signed autographs for them all. I would have signed a hundred more for the gratitude I felt.

Meanwhile, Ted had roused the garage man, and by the time the soldiers had their autographs, the car was ready. We drove off in one direction, the truck in the other—both exceedingly pleased by our meeting.

In 1938 I was invited to sing at a benefit for the Philadelphia Orchestra under the direction of Leopold Stokowski. I felt a little overawed at the thought of singing operatic arias in such august company, but I reflected that operatic singers and orchestral musicians enjoy performing swing and popular music, so why shouldn't I do it the other way around?

I chose an aria from Puccini's *La Bohème* and learned it, as I learn every song I sing, by listening to the music. When we were rehearsing with Mr. Stokowski, however, I found that there was a passage I was not completely sure of. When the orchestra stopped, I turned to Mr. Stokowski who was standing on the podium above me and asked him to whistle the passage for me.

There was a slight murmur of amusement among the members of the orchestra at so unorthodox a request to the Maestro, but Mr. Stokowski merely looked at me and said, "I beg your pardon, Miss Smith?"

I didn't hesitate—whistling a phrase was to me an accurate and legitimate way to get it right. "Please would you mind whistling that part for me because I'm not very familiar with it?" I asked.

His tone was very polite as he answered, "Shall we

give you a better light so you can read the notes, Miss Smith?"

"No, the light is perfectly all right," I told him. "I just can't read music."

He looked at me again for a moment and said, "You don't read music?" I expected him to throw his arms in the air and dismiss me with a grand gesture, but I had to admit it.

"Then do you learn by ear, Miss Smith?"

I confessed that I did, wondering what would happen then. To my surprise, his face broke into a smile.

"Don't ever take a lesson, Miss Smith. Your voice is a gift from God and should never be spoiled."

With that, he obligingly pursed his lips and whistled the passage for me.

During my second year on radio, CBS moved me from the seven o'clock time which had been so lucky for me and scheduled my program for a half hour later. In my place at seven o'clock a young man was being given his big chance. He had a lazy, slow voice, completely relaxed and relaxing. On his first program, which I heard at CBS, he was very nervous indeed, just as I had been, and he fumbled on his lyric. The words came out with a "boo-boo-boo" effect as he stumbled. As so often in show business, an accident proved to be the making of a star, for the public was fascinated by the new sound: Bing Crosby was on his way.

Throughout my career I have been extraordinarily lucky with reviewers and critics, who have on the whole treated me with kindness, understanding my motives as an entertainer. But there were two unpleasant incidents, one near the beginning of my career, and the other very recent.

During our hour-long shows on radio, we used a pool of actors to take small parts in the dramatic excerpts we presented each week. One of these actors wrote a song which he considered to be good enough for me to sing in public. Ted is extremely fair about choosing new songs, and has one criterion by which he judges them all, no matter who writes them: is it a good song? In his opinion, this song was not good, and on those grounds alone he turned it down.

Shortly after this, the actor married a gossip columnist on one of the New York newspapers. An unkind review appeared and many unpleasant remarks were made about me in this woman's column. It was obvious that they were motivated simply by spite; the actor clearly believed Ted had objected to his song on the grounds that he had written it, not that it was bad in itself.

I was the victim of another piece of spite when a recent program of ours had its premiere. A West Coast critic wrote "The balloon went up again last night," as the opening sentence of his review. Afterward, however, we discovered that he was involved in a quarrel with the network for which I was singing, and this was his method of getting revenge.

Ted and I believe that reviewers should concern themselves solely with the show they are asked to watch. They should ask themselves, "Was this a pleasant and rewarding few minutes of entertainment?" and should answer this question honestly, regardless of personal feelings toward the performers.

Nevertheless, I am always delighted when I get good reviews because they show that I am doing a good job. They are like a word of praise given to anyone trying his best. They encourage me to go on trying even harder. I was very pleased that when I returned to television on a weekly program in January, 1960, I received forty-six favorable reviews from all over the United States.

When people stop me on the street or in a store to tell me they like my program, I feel this is the greatest compliment of all. After all, I'm singing for people in their own homes, and if I please them, my job is really well done. They're the ultimate critics.

I have worked with most of the well-known names in the world of popular music during my career: Nat Brandwyn and Ted Straeter both played the piano for me for many years, and among those who played in our orchestra were Jimmy and Tommy Dorsey, Bunny Berigan, Will Bradley, Jack Jenny, and Charlie Spivack. We gave these musicians a chance to climb the ladder, but there was one we didn't give a chance. He was a second trombonist who wanted to be a singer. We felt that this desire of his was a bit like the comedian's hankering to play Hamlet, and besides, he was an excellent trombonist. He would come up to Ted and plead with him, rolling his big eyes and letting out strange, sustained sounds. But we always said "No."

We could have kicked ourselves when Bob Hope finally gave in and allowed Jerry Colonna to sing on one of his programs!

The secret of the enduring relationship between Ted as my manager and myself as a singer has always been his belief in my talent. I have heard him say, "If you want a popular song sung the way the composer intended, Kate's the greatest."

He really believes it, so much so that he has never undertaken the management of any other artist. "One is all I can handle," he always says. Over the years he has evolved methods of handling me which guarantee us that he will get what he wants and that I will be happy about it—no mean feat where a woman is concerned! Once he chose a song which I didn't like at first. I rehearsed it diligently, but I wasn't happy with it, and finally I said to him, "Ted, why am I singing this song?"

He smiled understandingly. "Okay, Kathryn, I won't schedule it again. But did you ever hear Sinatra sing it on the radio? He does it great!"

That was enough for me. I went right on and sang the

song as hard as I could, and it eventually became one of my favorites. Ted knew that the thought that another artist could do a song better than I could would be enough to pique my pride.

In the spring of 1960 I recorded a single song from the Broadway show "Greenwillow." After we had cut the record, Ted said to me casually, "Kathryn, did you know you sang that song in five octaves?"

I didn't know. Ted had worked closely with the arranger, as he always does, and had made the most of the tune. He didn't tell me beforehand what a task was facing me, because he knew that it was better for me not to know what might have worried me and spoiled my performance.

When I look back over thirty years in radio and television, I remember so many talented people who worked with us: Fannie Brice and Al Jolson appeared on our program in the thirties; Eddie Cantor, Jack Benny, George Burns and Gracie Allen all did guest spots for us; in our dramatic excerpts every week we gave a chance to Lee J. Cobb, Elia Kazan, Joseph Cotten, John Garfield, Orson Welles, Frank Lovejoy, Paul Stuart, and Everett Sloane, some of whom were making their first appearance in radio. Helen Hayes appeared on a Friday night hour-long show, as did Tyrone Power, Don Ameche, Henry Hull, and Brian Aherne.

Some people, reminiscing about the great performers they have known in the past, would say, "They don't come like that today!" But I don't say this. I feel that in spite of the great talents I have seen, we have only scratched the surface of potential talent in this country. This nation loves singing and loves acting. Every small town has its dramatic group, every club its barber-shop quartet, every home has music in one form or another. Most of the people who sing and act do so for their own pleasure and that of their friends and family, but some have wider ambitions. They can't resist the urge to go to New York and try their luck, pitting their talent against the huge odds of the big city. From these people who are willing to risk so much will come even greater entertainers than the ones I have known.

I have tremendous confidence in the future of show business because I believe that young people will always be willing to try for that big break, as I myself tried. There is today a great emphasis on security, and indeed it is a most desirable thing, but we should not forget that too much of it stifles ambition. If young people wish to risk insecurity for greater things, they should be encouraged to do so, for among them we shall find our new singers and great actors.

By the way, Kate Smith can't tell the story of her life without telling about a friend. During the 1940's and the early 1950's I had a thoroughly adorable and entirely spoiled cocker spaniel, whose name was Freckles and who struck terror into all new visitors to our apartment and to the house at Lake Placid, causing us hours of amusement. He was given to me one night at the

Columbia Playhouse when we were putting on our hour-long Friday night show. He was then a cream-colored lump of misery, for he was only a few weeks old and very sick. I nursed him night and day for the next few weeks, until he became strong and mischievous. Eventually his hair grew long and he was a very handsome creature. He was utterly devoted to me. Ted, who very tolerantly put up with him and his demands on my time, says that he was a one-woman dog. He was even present during our noontime broadcasts from the apartment, until one day he caused an uproar by rushing from the room barking loudly, pulling the microphone cable as he did so and causing the mike to crash to the floor. He was banished after that for the duration of each broadcast. His welcome to me when I came home after a show was like a small hurricane; at Lake Placid he would lie on the very edge of the dock waiting for my motor boat to come across the lake, and when he saw it, he set up such a barking that he could be heard all over the valley. He meant so much to me that when he died I had him buried in a cemetery where I put up a small headstone for him. I never had another dog. This small mention of him is merely my memorial to Freckles.

Eight

AFTER Ted's heart attack, his recovery was slow. Five anxious weeks were to pass before the oxygen tent was removed and he began to look more like himself. But it was not until twenty weeks had passed—in the middle of May—that he finally returned to his home from Doctors' Hospital. He was by then a shadow of the man he had been; he was much thinner, his face was without color, and he was under very strict medical orders.

On the day he came out of the hospital, I thanked Our Lady of New York on my knees that my prayers had been answered. I continued to go twice a day into the Cathedral, for I now felt I must keep my promise to Our Lady since she had been so very good to me.

Before Ted came out of the hospital, Mother and I had been up to Lake Placid to open my house. When he was able to travel, about the middle of June, Ted was taken up there to recuperate in his favorite spot—the house he had built in 1947.

It was a beautiful summer. The sunlight seemed even brighter, the water bluer. Mother and I visited Ted often. None of us did very much but live as quietly as we could, while the peacefulness of our surroundings put strength back into us. We enjoyed the Placid routine of life; I swam slowly in the lake in the mornings, Ted spent a lot of time at his fishing shack on the other side of the island. Mother and I went into the village to do our marketing and see friends. We had our usual visitors; my sister and my nieces came often, and all of us were refreshed by the normalcy of our lives. I hated to think what that summer might have been like, if Ted's illness had turned out differently.

Shortly after Labor Day, when I was enjoying the last really warm days of summer, Ted stopped by. The long vacation had improved him so that he looked almost as well, if not quite as vigorous, as he had been before that day in January. I could tell he was getting restless. The end of summer made him want to get busy again. He sat down on the patio steps.

"We'll soon have to be thinking about what you're going to do this season, Kathryn," he said, turning to me where I sat in a rocking chair.

"Why should we do anything?" I asked. "Doctor Garlan says you should rest for at least a year."

"I know, but you mustn't stay out of things too long. You know you'd rather be active. How long do you think you'd like not singing, not working? Besides, offers keep coming. Now I think I should start thinking of a weekly television spot——"

"Are you out of your mind, Ted? I think you'd be asking for another heart attack if we were to start a weekly series now."

"Aw, there isn't much work in a weekly show, you know—just a couple of days' choosing material and taping before the cameras."

"Why do you want to do it, Ted? Do you or I need the money?"

"No, of course not. No checks would bounce if you never sang another note for the rest of your life." He sat up suddenly. "But, Kathryn, you're an entertainer. Working's been your whole life. If you don't want to work right now, you will later on. You'll go out of your mind with nothing to do. And don't worry about me, Kate. Best thing in the world for me is work——"

I got equally firm about my point of view. "Will anything matter if you're dead? While you were ill, I used to wonder if it was all worth it. We worked so hard and so long, Ted. Look, we were on the radio every day for all those years, and then we were on television five days a week for four years. For what? So you could have a heart attack? No, Ted, I will not allow you to risk it. For the first time in my life I'm going to oppose you flatly—I will not do a weekly show this season."

"Okay, okay. Maybe next year will be time enough for that."

"I don't want ever to do anything regular again if it will affect your health, Ted."

"Well, what about a few guest appearances?" I began to bridle, but he lifted a hand and stopped me. "Make a compromise with me, Kathryn. I'll give up all ideas of a weekly show, but I would like you to do a few spots on other people's shows, just to keep you before the public. That won't hurt me, and you'll love it. Now how about it?"

I agreed, realizing that perhaps inactivity was as bad for Ted as too much activity. Ted had a satisfied grin on his face; I continued to rock in my chair, not completely happy. Although he was right that as a singer I probably would not be able to keep away from the stage, I didn't want his health further impaired. In any case, I had enjoyed twenty-five good years. But I smiled to myself when I realized that Ted was as much wedded to show business as I was. He too would find time heavy on his hands if he had no show to plan, no songs to choose. I guess he's just not the type to retire, and neither am I.

When I returned to New York a few weeks later, arrangements were made for me to make the appearances with the Ed Sullivan show that I should have made during Ted's illness. They were spaced out at long intervals, so that I was doing some of them a year later than we had originally planned.

But Ted was completely right when he said that having nothing to do would worry me, for the few appearances I made were so far apart that they became like great events to be prepared for and eagerly awaited, instead of routine jobs. Between them, I was plagued, for the first time in my life, with more hours than I could fill. Instead of waking each morning wondering how I was going to find the energy for all the things I had to do, now I would lie awake in the mornings and speculate on what I would find to do that day. To those who work hard every day, such a situation may seem very pleasant, but they too would soon see that too much freedom is just as great a burden as too many claims on one's time.

I would do a little shopping, taking my time selecting more items than I really needed. I would plan a special dish for dinner and spend as much time as possible cooking it exactly according to the recipe. I would go for walks in Central Park, and do all the things New Yorkers forget to do in their own city. My sister would visit me and we would go to the theater. Mother and I would take trips in the car to visit friends and relatives. I would spend a whole afternoon wandering in and out of my favorite antique shops. I watched television and listened to the radio. I redecorated my apartment.

But none of this was urgent. It was activity for the sake of activity, not for any ultimate end, and therefore had something hollow about it. When I asked myself why I was doing a certain thing, the answer was "Well, you've got to do something to get yourself tired." No one else's welfare depended on what I was doing, and the realization that this was the case began to depress me.

I found myself calling up Phyllis and Barbara more than ever, asking them to go to a matinee with me, to play cards, to go shopping. Phyllis was usually busy and could make only our evening dates to play gin rummy, but Barbara very frequently came to my Park Avenue apartment.

She had been a pretty girl in 1929, and now after twenty-seven years of marriage she was still handsome. She had light brown curls without a gray hair in them, and her face was round and nearly always had a smile.

One afternoon we sat in my apartment drinking tea and looking out of the window. Mother was in Connecticut on a visit. I had asked Barbara to keep me company. We came to a pause in the conversation and Barbara put her cup down.

"You know, Kate, I think something's wrong with you. You don't chatter as you used to."

I smiled at her. "I guess it's because there isn't so much to chatter about."

"Come on, admit it—you're bored, you haven't enough to do."

I looked at her with relief; I had been feeling guilty about my lack of occupation, and her frankness was a surprise.

"Don't feel bad about it, Kate. It's only natural. You've been answering cues so long, you're lost without working. Admit it, Kate, you're an old work-horse, a ham, maybe—and you want to be back there in front of a camera singing your heart out and having fun!"

"Maybe you're right, Barbara."

"Of course I am. The same goes for me. I miss being constantly in demand by my family—I don't have nearly enough to do."

"Barbara, I thought married women always had their hands full. Haven't you?"

She shook her head. "No. In fact, I haven't enough to do either these days and that's why I thought I'd talk it over with you. Since my daughter got married last year——"

I interrupted. "You know something? I was talking over her wedding present with Mother when I heard about Ted's illness."

"Yes, and oddly enough Ted's heart attack played the same part in your life as the wedding did in mine. It put us both out of work—out of having enough work to do, that is. You see, Roger'll be out of college this summer, and he hasn't been at home much for the past three years anyway."

I asked about looking after her house.

"Kate, after twenty-seven years, that house runs it-

self. It's too big for the two of us, anyway. We're thinking of renting it and taking an apartment."

"So here you are, your daughter married and in California, and your son not living at home. What about
your husband? He must take some looking after."

She laughed. "He isn't home for lunch, and we like to
dine out quite often and go on to a show. Besides, I
know his tastes and his moods so that I don't have to
ask him about anything—I can sense what he wants to
eat and wants to do!"

"So what happens now?"

She sighed. "That's the trouble. And that's what's
bothering you too. Because you were forced to retire—
at least as much as you will ever retire—at the same
stage of life as the average married woman finds herself
with her children grown up, you know just how I feel."

"Well, if it's anything like how I feel, with time hang-
ing on my hands, it's not pleasant. You know, I want to
feel of use to someone again. I'd like to get that feeling
of being part of a team, the way you are in a television
show or behind a microphone."

"Or the way I felt as I sat at the dinner table and
looked at my family."

"I'd like to feel I have to be somewhere at a certain
time," I continued.

Barbara nodded. "Just as I'd like to feel I have to get
breakfast at a certain time or the kids would be late for
school. I'd like to feel useful."

We looked at each other, and said, almost in unison, "Well, what do we do about it?" We laughed, and I poured more tea for each of us.

"What did our mothers and grandmothers do about it?" I mused.

Barbara answered enthusiastically. "That's the interesting thing about this situation—it's almost entirely a problem facing our generation." Her brown hair shone as she put the cup down to leave her hands free for gesticulation. "You see, until now the life expectancy of a woman wasn't too high—although it's always been higher for women than men—so that all she could expect from life was to rear her children and then die. She couldn't expect to see her grandchildren beyond infancy, if that. And she was so worn out with all the heavy household work which raising a family meant in those days that she was glad to rest for the few remaining years of her life. But now, women live a great deal longer and they have their children earlier. We live longer than men. In fact, most married women now have to look forward to spending the last years of their lives as widows."

"And they call men the stronger sex," I smiled. "Outliving them is not an ideal arrangement."

"You used to talk about the subject a lot on the air, remember?"

"You know, Ted and I had some great fun arguing the matter on our noontime programs in the forties.

But how come you know so much about middle-aged women with little to do, Barbara?"

"Because I'm one of them. I got interested in the problem when it first began to hit me and I started reading what I could find about it. I wish I'd looked into the matter sooner."

"But you've only just become really free. Your daughter wasn't married till last year."

"Yes, but if I'd had the sense to see what was going to happen to me in advance, I could have started preparing ten years ago. I could have taken courses while the children were in high school and taken a job when Roger went to college three years ago."

"You really think you would have taken a job, at your time of life?"

"Kate, boredom makes you older quicker than any responsibility could. It is a bit late now, but I may still do it. I might go back to school and to work. And you —you, Kate, sing again. Don't ever stop singing. Go on out there and snap your fingers and let go with that big voice. That's the answer to your problem."

From what I could find to read on the subject, I learned that the problem of middle-aged women had several aspects to it: it differed for women with college educations; and it was slightly different again for women with higher degrees than the A.B. In addition, there was another interesting aspect to work done by women over forty—women need work for their own welfare, but society needs the contribution of women because there is a continuing manpower shortage.

Certain general truths emerged, such as the curious fact that in the years between 1890 and 1950, the average age of first marriage for women in this country declined from twenty-two to twenty years. I couldn't see any reason why this should be, and no sociologists seem to be able to give completely satisfactory explanations. It is well known that people marry earlier in times of greater prosperity, but this country has only been very prosperous for the large mass of people since the last war. However, there it is—and the age for first marriage is still declining. The large number of high school brides is clear evidence of this.

Today's bride of twenty generally has her last child by the time she is twenty-six years old. By the time she's thirty-two, all of her children will be in school, and when she's in her forties, they'll all be ready to fly from the nest. And mother faces thirty more years of life with time, not children, on her hands. Just as the number of children in this country is increasing, so is the number of older people and especially older women.

Among the material I read was a report of the inaugural address by the new president of Mt. Holyoke College, Richard Gettell. I remembered reading the speech at the time it was given in 1957, because since I met Dr. Woolley, a former president of the college, in the thirties, I had always been interested in Mt. Holyoke. It was the first woman's college in this country, and I found that it was leading the way again, for Mr. Gettell had pointed out that the lives of American women are beginning to take on a new pattern, a three-phased one instead of the former two-phased one. Men's lives have a two-phased pattern, consisting of training and then a career; formerly women's lives were divided up in the same way—training and then marriage. But, as Mr. Gettell says, "Woman's life is three-phased today: first, training and schooling, second, family and homemaking, third (since the children grow up and leave the family hearth while the mother is still at a relatively early age), the search for a vocation or avocation." He goes on to say that of course there are many variations of this pattern, as for instance in cases where a woman keeps on with her career throughout her marriage. But basically the three-phased pattern is the one which is emerging and which presents a challenge to education and to employers.

As I read this, I wondered whether, had I been young in the sixties of this century instead of the thirties, my life would have been different. Would I, perhaps, have had both a marriage and a career? Would I have married my operatic tenor and returned to singing when our brilliant children were studying music in college? Who knows?

Mr. Gettell was, of course, most concerned about the effect of this pattern on the college-educated girl—and upon the education the college should give the girl. He raises the question of the best curriculum for a college girl who is unlikely to work for very long after she graduates, a girl who will marry soon after graduation and occupy herself with the chores of a home and a family. He thinks that a liberal arts course of the widest possible scope would train a girl to think for herself, and keep her sufficiently alive to intellectual interests so that she can take them up again when she wants to work in middle age. Then, too, he suggests that alumnae might be helped with reading lists and bulletins to keep them up-to-date on developments in their field of study so that adjustments when they go to work will not be so hard. He recommends refresher courses for older women, and a number of colleges are already experimenting with them.

I wonder myself whether we don't need a completely radical approach to the whole field of women's education. I'm not an expert, of course, but I do feel strongly that we should educate women as women, and if the pattern of women's lives is changing, then the pattern of education should change too. To this end, it might be even better than the present system if a girl's four-year college course were divided into two parts, two years to be completed when she is young, and two years to be taken when she is thirty-eight or forty, when her children can look after themselves to a certain extent. The degree would not be given her until she had completed her four years; because it would bring her back into the discipline of learning, it would eliminate the need for refresher courses before she goes out to work again. In my Utopian scheme, I see a girl going away to college as she so frequently does now, and remaining there for two years, with the idea of not marrying during that time. Then, after she has married and brought up her children, she could go to another college in the town where she and her husband live, a college affiliated with her original one and carrying credits from it. Going to school and keeping house at the same time would present no problems to an experienced housekeeper. Because of her greater maturity, she would be more likely to concentrate on her studies, and it's perfectly possible she would get more out of her last two years of college at the age of forty than she would at the age of twenty. Of course, other girls who had no interest in getting married early would take the normal four years of college. They would be the ones most likely to go on to an advanced degree in any case.

The main problem my plan presents, quite apart from its practical difficulties which are obviously many, is the attitude of the general public to mature women going to school. In fact, public opinion is the main stumbling block to any solution of the problem of middle-aged women and their boredom. What people will say is a force to be reckoned with, but people's opinions take so much longer than sociology and economics to catch up with changing trends. There will be people who will sneer at women taking courses and learning new skills at forty or older. But this is a new problem requiring a new approach and old objections cannot stand in the way.

The women who did not go to college, as a rule, marry even earlier and have their children off their hands before they can be called middle-aged. They find jobs of a different kind from those which attract college-educated women, but I see no reason why they too shouldn't go back to school. After all, a woman who has spent twenty years looking after a husband and family might regret not having gone to college when she was young and might like to go when she has more time to devote herself to her studies. I am aware that there are many adult education courses, but I would like to see people approaching them in a quite different spirit from that of the dilettante; instead of saying to herself that she's taking up something to kill time, a woman should feel she's preparing herself for a career. Since she's probably going to be working until the age of sixty or sixty-five, those years deserve proper preparation.

When a woman of forty or forty-five just "wants a job" and doesn't want to go back to school before getting it, she often runs into difficulty as a result of the attitude of employers. In a recent study published by the National Manpower Council, researchers found that many employers had a prejudice against employing women over thirty or thirty-five. They put forward such objections as a feeling that middle-aged women were too set in their ways to adapt; they were difficult to get on with because they wouldn't mix with younger people; they tended to be timid and preferred "blind-alley" type jobs to launching out into new fields. All this may be true, but there's another side to the coin, as employers who were more broad-minded discovered. Middle-aged women have greater stability, they are more loyal, and their capacity for steady work is greater than that of younger women.

It is necessary, of course, to develop greater flexibility on the part of the employer. The study, which is appropriately entitled *Womanpower*, points out that a great deal could be done in exploring the possibilities of part-time work; the attitude should be one of adapting the job to the woman as well as the woman to the job. Employers who take the trouble to see how they can suit a woman's convenience in working hours often find an unexpectedly large return in loyalty and performance.

Women who have higher degrees than the normal four-year college education could be extremely valuable to society during the present—and increasing—shortage of college teachers. Radcliffe College made a complete study of its alumnae who had taken Ph.D. degrees and found that there was a considerable amount of talent going to waste among those who had married and finished raising their families. One woman said:

"During the past twenty years I have limited myself to volunteer occupations and to study, research and some writing. Now at forty-five, with the last two children soon to go away to school, I am eager to do some full-time teaching as well as research. My work at the University since 1947 should provide an up-to-date refresher. A Ph.D. education, good health, a lot of community experience, a love of teaching and twenty years to go to normal retirement—these, I hope, will be considered useful assets somewhere in the field of higher education. If one of the goals of modern education for girls is training for good citizenship, a married Ph.D.'s experience in family and community might be interpreted as an added qualification for teaching, but in general I find it a handicap. I cannot at the moment round out my account of my personal experience as a married Ph.D. and how the problem of re-entry into the academic field was solved, because the final chapter is not yet lived. I hope that final chapter is one of academic life again."

Nothing could more clearly illustrate my point that public and employer opinion often defeat society's best interests with a prejudice against middle-aged women. Here is a woman who has clearly not only kept up her interest in her subject during the time her family was growing up, but has obviously benefited from her experience as a mother and become a mature, well-balanced person. And she is willing and eager to give the best of her own learning to others by teaching. But she encounters college administrators who consider her experience as a wife and mother a handicap to her ability to teach.

There is a tendency for the teaching faculties of

women's colleges to consist of more and more men, because the women who might be staffing them leave and get married so early. Men may be equally good as teachers for women, but I should not have thought a better teacher for girls could be found than a woman such as the Radcliffe Ph.D. above. Since there is a lack of teachers, I hope women's colleges will make real efforts to utilize to the full the women who would like to make a "comeback" at forty.

Barbara's point that a woman's boredom shows in her face and her manner was also taken up by researchers in a report issued by the American Council on Education, entitled "How Fare American Women?" They say:

"The ability of women over forty to make constructive and satisfying use of leisure time and to contribute productively to society at this stage of life will directly affect their own adjustment as well as that of their husbands and children."

I should think a woman who is interested in work outside her home would be a better companion for her husband than one who is continually bored and complaining about it. She would feel bound to dress well, to look after her figure, and to keep herself as young as possible, all tasks which would be made simpler because of the competitive stimulus of being with other people. We may eventually find that if large numbers of women do take up new interests after forty, their marriages will also benefit from a return to conditions like those when both partners were young.

Of course one of the major difficulties is that women themselves have so far not been aware of the new pattern of their lives. What young girl of eighteen can look forward across the years to herself at forty and plan accordingly? But society needs the womanpower middle-aged women can provide. There are going to be more and more jobs for women—already electronics assembly is almost exclusively a feminine occupation—as we go into the age of the atom. The Manpower Council made two recommendations when it finished its researches for *Womanpower*. First it proposed that "Federal and state governments, employers, unions and voluntary organizations should cooperate to increase occupational guidance and placement services for mature women who want to work."

It also recommended that these authorities should "initiate surveys to determine whether existing training facilities are adequate to meet the needs of mature women who want to work, and in what ways mature women can be helped to meet the requirements for employment where manpower shortages exist."

Barbara and I were talking our researches over with Phyllis a few weeks later. I pointed out to Barbara that I'd enjoyed reading the books and pamphlets so much that I felt it was an occupation in itself.

"You see what I mean?" said Barbara. "You need something to take yourself out of yourself. In your case just looking at a new problem helped, so think what a new job would do for a lot of women."

Phyllis broke in. "Yes, but I think you've both forgotten one very important aspect of the situation."

She waited for one of us to say "Which one?" and so I obliged.

"Volunteer work is what I mean," she went on. "What about the thousands of women who devote their time to raising money for charities, to helping with political campaigns, to visiting in hospitals? I remember when I was nursing in hospitals here in New York how useful the women were who came in for a few hours a day and helped give the patients their meals."

"Yes, I know," answered Barbara, "but how much of that is just 'busy' work—doing something for the sake of doing something?"

Phyllis seemed a little taken aback. "I think a lot of people would resent that."

"I'm sorry, I wasn't expressing myself well," said Barbara, a little more slowly. "What I mean is, I think a woman who wants to make herself useful needs to feel that what she is doing is something real. She doesn't want to be playing at things. And no matter how they may talk about it, volunteer workers have essentially a dilettante attitude."

"Well, I do see what you mean. I know many people who serve on committees not because of what they can do to help but because of what the work does for them."

"Yes, that's it. That's why I feel that I personally

would like to be doing a proper daily job with specified hours and rate of pay, and know that if I didn't do it well, I would be criticized as I should be, instead of having people worrying about hurting my feelings because I mightn't come again."

"Yes," I put in, "so that you get the reality of a challenge and of the possibility of failure."

"Do you have any ideas about what you'd like to do, then?" Phyllis asked Barbara.

"I've been wondering about that, although I think it's a bit late for me now. If I had my time over again, though, I'd be a kindergarten school teacher now. I would have taken training while my two children were in their last years at school, and then have taken a job as soon as they left home for college."

"That sounds perfect," I said to her. "Who could be better at it? You've brought up two of your own—and what could be more satisfying?"

"It would have been great. And I have more patience now than I ever had as a young woman."

Phyllis said, "It would also be perfect from the point of view of your husband, because you'd be off from work during the summer and could be with him when he took his vacation."

"Why not do it now?" I suggested.

"I don't see how I could. By the time I was through training I'd be over fifty, and in spite of what I think, I know a lot of school principals think that's too old to begin."

We fell silent. "What a shame!" said Phyllis after a pause. "And that must be happening to so many women."

"Yes. I guess I'll just have to spend my time warning younger women not to make the mistake I made. Be a kind of evangelist for the cause," Barbara said with a laugh.

"Why not take some courses in something for your own amusement? You know, learn clay modeling or basket weaving," I said, without much hope.

"No, Kate. Don't you see? That's just what I don't want to do. I don't want to whip up any artificial enthusiasm for something. I want to feel that what I'm doing is absolutely vital to someone and that I've got to do a good job or someone else would suffer. That's why teaching would have been such a good idea, for this country needs as many teachers as it can get."

Phyllis had the last word. "Well, if you go around telling people what you've discovered about the problem of women over forty with nothing to do, you won't be wasting your time. You've already made two more people—Kate and me—worry about it. Just think how many more you can get talking by the end of the year!"

Nine

$\mathcal{B}$ E C A U S E of my guest appearances on programs like the Ed Sullivan, Tennessee Ernie, and Perry Como shows, I was not free to take up anything new in the way of a career or job, even if I really had been able to do anything else besides sing. So, like Barbara, I decided to put on a brave face toward my boredom and the two of us made a hobby of looking for items in newspapers and magazines about what was being done to defeat our problem. It was a substitute, we both knew, for what we would really like to do.

Meanwhile Ted, obeying his doctor's orders, was taking life quietly, except when we had a show to do. Whenever I sing, he is in the control room. There is far more behind the rendition of a song medley than the average viewer realizes. Ted works hard to make my segment of the show a part of the entire presentation. This is not only out of respect for the show and the person in charge but in the interest of good programming. When I come as a guest to another person's program I try to fit in with his other guests and go along with his plan of entertainment. Good showmanship is first of all a matter of good taste.

Although I can sing a song a dozen different ways it's Ted who knows, even more than I do, exactly how that song should sound coming from me. Sometimes we've experimented for fun in recording sessions and I've put on a bit of an act for the musicians and for Ted to show them I can sing a song in the styles of a variety of singers. I belt out a number or do it blues style or even imitate some of the famous men singers. Yes, I'm that much of a ham. Ted gets a big kick out of it but always insists that I sing the song in my own way because, "That's the 'sound' the folks expect from you, Kathryn."

Ted's relaxation for many months took the form of watching television; he became the only person I knew who followed daytime serials on TV. He watched them out of bewildered curiosity, I think, and was amazed and amused and often indignant. I couldn't watch them because they annoyed me after a very short time, but he found them absorbing and extremely funny, often because different actors frequently took over the same roles in successive episodes. A character would look entirely different—a husband would change from being tall and dark to short and fair, for instance, or a man accused of a crime would undergo a metamorphosis between the police precinct and the trial. Ted would expatiate at length on these serials, with such a wealth of comic observation that my mother and I would laugh until the tears rolled down our cheeks.

He became exceedingly critical of the unending diet of Western shows which was fed to the public during 1958 and 1959. He used to say, "I can't put the TV set on in the evenings without seeing a horse charge across the screen from right to left. And in the next program, the same horse is going from left to right. You'd think those paths in the desert would be worn down to bedrock with the number of cowboys who ride over them every evening."

But as 1959 wore on, he was worried not so much by the Westerns as by the slick crime dramas which were becoming more and more popular. When Ted came over for dinner one evening he insisted that I watch one of the shows with him. A number of men in immaculate dinner jackets seemed to be plotting a crime. There was a fight in which some of the men watched others brutally beating up an adversary; streams of blood dripped from the man's face to the floor and bullets whizzed across the screen. We sat appalled for a few moments and then Ted got up and abruptly switched off the set.

"That's vicious stuff, Kathryn. Just think what it must be doing to young people, what ideas it must be putting into their heads. If they knew nothing about killing before, that'll soon teach them."

"I wouldn't like that kind of thing corrupting my children," I said.

"I'm surprised there isn't more juvenile delinquency than there is," Ted fumed. "Anything you put on television is automatically glorified. Why go to college if a guy with a gun can outsmart you?"

"Is there anything on another channel we can watch?"

"No, that's the worst of it. Here, take a look." He handed me the television page of the newspaper. "Every channel you turn to has either this or a Western. And that's another thing," he said, tapping the arm of his chair for emphasis, "even the Westerns have this brutal stuff now. The plots have nothing to do with the West or with ranching. You could just put the same actors in business suits and give them the same lines, and nobody would know the difference. Even the horses are there only for decoration."

What really disturbed us most was that television, a marvelous medium more powerful than any means of communication ever before known, is not used more for the greatest good. We're not against good entertainment in *any* field—mystery, detective, romance, or variety. We are against bad taste, endless imitation, lack of experimentation, over-production, and the disrespect shown to the public by many who have power in the television business but neither the talent nor the faith in the public they should have. We deplore the idea that seems to have become a credo for too many people in television —that the interests of the general public are on an exceedingly low level.

Certainly in our years of radio and television we expressed ideas and views in simple terms, but not because we felt that the general public is moronic. Since the beginning of time and the written word great truths can and have been told in simple terms. The Bible is the best example of this. The Gettysburg Address is magnificent in its simplicity. The Constitution of the United States and the United Nations Charter are not veiled in mystifying terms. And we ourselves had proof in millions of letters over the years that people respond to honest, realistic, and factual messages, entertainment, and stimulating ideas.

We don't say that there is nothing good being done in television. In its brief history, and even when it had to struggle with economics, as any new industry must, there have been some inspiring and exciting programs— just enough to make viewers realize the vital and tremendous potential of the medium. And enough, too, to make viewers sad that so much talent and enthusiasm on the part of many genuinely sincere performers and producers is either being ignored or wasted.

A relatively small handful of people have proven that documentaries can be highly entertaining as well as informative. These heroes and heroines are far more unsung than many who have contributed nothing but mechanical, brutal images to the television screens of the nation. Those who have labored with their hearts and their abiding faith in the public have had rather small rewards. Perhaps you, as a viewer, are somewhat to blame. Do you make yourself heard when you see a fine program as well as when your indignation is expressed about a bad one? Do you ever sit down and write the network, the local station, the producer or the performer when a worthwhile show has been presented? We're all probably remiss on that score.

I've heard some cynics say that radio reached its height during and because of the war. True, radio achieved the greatest measure of its capacity in those years but I will never be convinced that it took a war to do it. Television does not need a war to prove its worth. Peace is a greater challenge which television can and must meet.

Ted sighed. "I don't know what it's coming to. And the worst of it is, Kathryn, that this junk sells. Look at the way sponsors clamor to get on these smart crime shows—sponsors that you and I know wouldn't have wanted their goods connected with such filth fifteen years ago. Let's listen to some songs."

He got up and went to the tape-recorder. Soon the apartment was filled with my voice singing a medley of songs we had both loved for many years. The sound of my own voice no longer startles me, of course, but whenever I hear it I get more and more critical; I am always sure I could have sung a song just that little bit better.

The songs didn't soothe Ted very much, for he soon started grumbling again. "And there's another thing about television—there isn't a straight musical show on either."

"What do you mean? There are quite a lot of singing stars who have their own shows."

"Sure, but they pad them out with so many guests doing such things as balancing balls on their noses or riding bicycles on high wires while playing the accordion. And comedians. And dancers. Nobody trusts straight music, just good music any more."

During the year following Ted's heart attack I had cause to worry about my own health. Dr. Garlan eventually told me that if I didn't lose weight my own heart would be in danger; I already had symptoms of hypertension. My doctor reminded me that I would have to take the weight off slowly, since I had put it on over a period of years. By limiting myself to a diet of 1,000 calories a day, of course under Dr. Garlan's supervision, I was able to lose 85 pounds in three years. And I found that there was no need for me to be hungry while on this diet. Many people find themselves submitting to excessive appetites without realizing that they do not need to eat so much food.

I had long been accustomed to using up tremendous energy while doing so many programs, and in addition I went beyond my actual need for food, since I would eat during rehearsals just because food was around. It was a question of breaking a habit, for I had no real need for the food I consumed at a time when I was far less active. I knew, too, that I would never be slim. I just wanted to be healthy.

The problem of having little to do was therefore intensified at first by the effort to break a habit. I would be able to pass one day following my diet with no trouble, but the next day I would suddenly think about cake. The thought wouldn't leave me. A slice of chocolate cake would become fixed in my mind, interposed between me and my other thoughts. It would become huge and monstrous, the biggest slice of chocolate cake in the world, its texture soft and perfect, its frosting succulent and deep brown. I could smell its aroma, and my mouth would begin watering. Finally I would give way, and practically run to the nearest lunch counter or cake shop. I would gulp it down as if it were vital to my existence and I had been on the point of death without it. And then I would suffer from remorse. I would eat nothing further that day and would go to bed with only a glass of tomato juice.

But by the end of 1958 I had fairly conquered my craving and was feeling better than I had felt in many years. I could pass a cake shop with only a cook's interest in the cakes displayed; I could pass up pie when I was offered it at a friend's house for dinner; and I no longer wanted ice cream. When you once lose the taste for sweet things, they seem cloying and unpleasant, and there's no difficulty in doing without them.

*

In the fall of 1959, Ted called me on the telephone one day and said, "Come on over, Kathryn. Got something I want to discuss with you."

When I got there and had taken my coat off, he took a long look at me as I stood in the middle of the room.

"You're looking younger than ever, Kathryn. You'll be sylph-like yet."

"Well, thanks, Ted, though that's a bit extreme. What's on your mind?"

"Got an offer for a weekly show, Kathryn, to start early next year. I think we can show them that a simply-produced musical show can be successful."

"A one-man clean-up campaign, eh? And what did Doctor Garlan say about your undertaking a series?"

"You're wrong—it's a one-woman campaign, because you're going to do all the hard work. And Garlan says I'm perfectly all right. In fact he thinks I'd probably be better off doing something regularly instead of nothing most of the time."

"Well, I'm going to check with him just to make sure." I tried to look grim and disapproving, but I caught Ted's eye and we both laughed for sheer joy. "Oh, Ted, I think it's wonderful. Nothing would make me happier than to go back to singing every week. I'm not sure that I look younger, but I certainly feel as young as I ever did and I'd just love to stand up there and sing at the top of my voice." I realized again how much I had missed my work."

"Fine. It'll certainly be good to be back in harness."

"What sort of show are you planning?"

"Just as much music as we can cram into half an hour. You'll sing new songs, there'll be a spot for old ones, we'll have a couple of guests who'll do nothing but make music—no acrobats. Simple backgrounds, clear lighting, an orchestra. The sort of thing we both like best."

"But what about the sponsors? I thought they preferred crime shows these days."

"We're doing pretty well in that department too. And you know something? I think the public's ready for a change."

"Ted, I've never known you wrong in your predictions of public taste. I don't see why you should be now. I'm looking forward to it."

"The nicest part of it as far as I'm concerned is that we're just doing it because we want to. We don't have to. If it fails we don't lose a thing and if it succeeds, we're just adding to our own as well as everyone else's pleasure. It's an ideal position to be in."

"But Ted——" I'd just remembered something.

"It's all right, Kathryn, I haven't forgotten your Christmas show and the other date with Ernie Ford out on the coast."

I suddenly saw before me all that would have to be done. "How can I fit it all in, Ted? I've got to go out to California, come back, then get dresses ordered, experiment with my hair every week, and then there's Christmas, and Florida in March, and we'll have to choose lots of songs——"

"Here we go again!" Ted laughed. "That's the old Kate Smith—too many things to do and not enough hours in the day!"

So my problem of not having enough to do was swept away in a sudden whirl of activity. A return to singing was really what I had always thought of as the best possible solution.

Ted and I had a great deal of fun choosing songs, for it meant going back over our twenty-nine years of music, always a pleasant thing to do. I was amazed when Ted told me I'd recorded over 2,200 songs in that time; I think we played most of them over on Ted's tape-recorder while we were planning the new series. Ted was the old work-horse again but he was more relaxed than in the old days. I was glad of that.

"I'm so glad we stuck to the best songs, Kathryn. I don't think you can beat songs by Irving Berlin, Jerome Kern, Cole Porter and all the others, the good standards."

"Don't forget I like jazz, too," I answered, listening to the tape and wondering if I'd got a certain beat just right.

"Sure, but that's part of the best American tradition too. You know, I think when people finally come to write the musical history of this century, they'll have to admit that America's great contribution was the popular

song—things like 'You're Driving Me Crazy,' 'Our Love
is Here to Stay,' 'Anything Goes.' Songs anybody can
whistle."

"They're certainly the best ones to sing. But I was
just wondering, Ted, aren't they a bit old-fashioned for
young people? I mean, if we're aiming our show at the
older generation, they'll go over fine, but young people
today seem to like rock 'n' roll."

He got up and went to change the tape. "Well, if they
do, that's their loss. Young people with any sense of a
good song will know the good tunes and love them as
much as anybody. And don't forget Tin Pan Alley still
turns out good things."

"Well, if you choose them for me I can bet they'll be
pretty near the standard of the old ones."

"And if you sing 'em straight as you've always done,
they'll be hits."

Ted and I have always maintained that the best way
to sing a song is as near to the composer's intentions as
possible. I don't depart from the basic melody. I don't
camouflage his theme with unnecessary, exaggerated variations. My first approach to a song is to listen to it as a
complete unit of verses and music. If it's a new song, I
get the composer to sit down at the piano to play and
sing it himself. If it's an old one, I listen to a record. I
want to form an impression of the song as a whole. I try
to enjoy it as anyone would who was hearing the song
for the first time.

Then I go away and think about the song, usually

with the words and music in my hand. I ask myself what I enjoyed in it, what made it unique. Does it have an appealing flow of melody, a poignant little twist of musical line? Or did I enjoy most of all the song's idea, maybe some sentiment near to my own heart? Or was it the rhythm that got me? Every song has one major attraction in its make-up, and that's what I work at first. I hum it over and over to myself, getting the feeling of what the composer intended as his song's main appeal. I shall always respect the composer. If I embellish, it is his idea I am embellishing.

When I'm familiar with the spirit of the song, I go back and work at its form. First comes pitch. Although I have no difficulty in keeping true to pitch, it is important that every note should hit a bull's-eye of clear, pure tonality, and I work at the tune not merely to learn it but to make it second nature.

Next comes rhythm, the heart-beat of every composition. I think that the average listener is consciously aware of rhythm only when it is strongly marked, as in a march or waltz. The singer, however, must go deeper than this. He must establish the pulse of the song. Never must it be allowed to lag or to run ahead, or deviate in any way from what the composer intended. Many popular singers today adapt the song to suit their personal style, instead of subordinating their style to what the composer wrote. Even when measures are accelerated or slowed up, the inner rhythmic pattern must not be allowed to vary.

Then there is enunciation. It is important that the audience should understand every syllable of every word, for only then can they grasp the meaning of the song and follow the shades of emotion behind it. Enunciation should be clear without being exaggerated. It is often helpful to me to recite the words, in natural speech, as though I were relating the events or emotions of a poem to a friend. When I'm rehearsing on the stage before we tape the Kate Smith Show, I often stand off at one side and recite the words of a new song to myself. This has two advantages, for not only is loose or slovenly enunciation corrected in this way, but also the significance of the words stands out as the foundation for the interpretation of the song. In nearly all ballads, the words set the mood and meaning, while the music intensifies or enhances them. That is why it is wise to begin work on a new song with a thorough study of the words.

In fourth place comes the musical interpretation itself, for the mood and feeling of the song must be carried into the hearts as well as the ears of the listeners. The first essential in capturing this feeling and then conveying it to the listener is complete sincerity. The ultimate result of all public performance is effect—the effect of the song and the singer on the listeners. Yet paradoxically any conscious striving after that effect means ruin. The effect upon the listener is gaged by the lack of conscious effect and the amount of genuine sincerity and

believability the singer can project. I am often asked
how I can sing all the varied types of songs I like so
much—blues, ballads, religious songs, rhythm numbers,
love songs—and sound equally sincere in them all. But
people who wonder about that forget that personal preference has nothing to do with sincerity in singing, or in
any other interpretive art. Intelligent analysis of the
composer's intention and strict adherence to it automatically ensure sincerity.

Every song contains a human message, and it is the
singer's task to search out that message and give it
back again to the audience. A blues song can express
essential sadness but so can a song by Schubert. I am
not implying that the sadness is expressed in the same
way—only that it is there. The intelligent singer dis-
covers this note of sadness and tries to respond to it, to
re-create it, to voice real human sympathy with it, and
so stimulate a like sympathy in the hearts of those who
listen. If I have a religious song to sing, I try to find and
experience the exaltation of religion. I remember how I
myself feel in church when the solemnity of the service
fills me with wonder and awe. Then I try to put that
feeling into my voice as I sing. When I'm singing a song
of cheerfulness and hope, I remember the good times
I've had and I sing with all the sense of joy I felt then.
The secret is living a song as part of my life. Exactly as
in life, I try to be quite sure what I'm feeling and then
be absolutely honest in my expression. In this way I can

sometimes get that wonderful sympathy between me and my audience, telling me I've reached their hearts. And believe me, when I do, the thrill is mine.

Of course, since I have been singing for so many years, I don't always need to approach a song quite so laboriously and meticulously, since the process has largely become second nature to me now. In fact, I can often record even a new song with only a matter of one or two runs through beforehand. But if there should be any difficulty, if the song isn't coming out as I want it to, I begin at the beginning of the process I've described and take every step. It hardly ever fails.

I am exceedingly lucky in that my voice, along with perfect pitch and perfect rhythm, was given me at birth. I learn my songs by ear; I breathe, focus my tones and resonate them without knowing why. I can repeat any song I've heard once, in its proper key, and I make all necessary transpositions by ear. My singing is part of me, like my stoutness, or my light hair, or my poor eyesight. Of course it seems unfair to other people that they should have to train for many years and practice hours and hours a day in order to sing, when I don't; I am continually embarrassed by people who point me out as an example of what can be done without training. But I feel my gifts as a responsibility, and I do not take them for granted. Because I approach my singing with a different equipment from performers who have spent many years in studying voice production, I feel that I must work hard to make my singing above reproach;

there must be no faults which hard work would take care of, and no liberties with the composer's intentions may be tolerated. I measure my interpretation of a song continually against my ideal of what the song should be. I am harder on myself than anyone else—even Ted— could be.

Let me say a word about rock-and-roll. Someone recently asked Ted, "How does Kate feel about rock-and-roll?"

"She loves it," he replied, surprising the newspaper interviewer.

If rock-and-roll is well done, by a voice that is neither manufactured nor has no music in it at all, and if the beat is executed correctly, there's nothing so terribly wrong with that kind of music. But the lyrics are another story. Certainly the lyrics have been, in many instances, ridiculous, revolting, and senseless. Perhaps it is because of such lyrics that parents and other critics have been against rock-and-roll. I'm not opposed to nonsensical lyrics—they can even be quite delightful. I believe you can sing "la-la-la" and make it effective and catching if the beat is done well. Don't forget I sang such songs as "Mairsy Doats," which isn't exactly great literature but was great fun. Honestly, I'd love to try a few rock-and-roll songs—which, in reality, are another variety of the various rhythm songs I do sing. But Ted thinks my audience doesn't want that from me. Well, it's up to the audience. It always has been.

A weekly TV show requires a full day before the cameras, with many rehearsals and then a final performance which is recorded on tape. But of course a great deal more goes into it than one day. Ted spends several other days a week planning and choosing backgrounds, selecting songs, approving scripts, arranging for our guests. He works hours and hours with all the other people involved. I devote at least one day a week to fittings for dresses. My hair is a constant problem. I'll tell you a secret. I'm a natural blonde but my natural blonde looks dull gray over television, so, believe it or not, I darken my hair, somewhat sadly, for the television camera.

Countless other details have to be attended to, but finally everything is centered on the stage at the television studio. For hours I stand before the cameras in my ordinary clothes while the director in the control room gets positions and lights right. For hours the chorus and the guests go over their performances, working with the orchestra to get exactly the effect which they want. Finally, we all break and go to dress, putting on the exaggerated make-up that television lighting requires; the men wear pale blue dress shirts and everyone's face is brick-red.

When we go back on stage, an audience is there, giving the atmosphere of excitement that will galvanize our performance. All is silence as we wait for Ted in the control room to say "okay." The orchestra starts the 1960 version of "When the Moon Comes Over the Mountain" and I'm singing again. I hope I always will be—not asking what the future holds, but being thankful for the present; content to work, to spread some happiness if I may, and always trying to be my best self.